Questions Preachers Ask

Questions Preachers Ask

Essays in Honor of Thomas G. Long

Edited by
Scott Black Johnston
Ted A. Smith
Leonora Tubbs Tisdale

WESTMINSTER
JOHN KNOX PRESS
LOUISVILLE · KENTUCKY

© 2016 Westminster John Knox Press

First edition
Published by Westminster John Knox Press
Louisville, Kentucky

16 17 18 19 20 21 22 23 24 25—10 9 8 7 6 5 4 3 2 1

Unless otherwise indicated, Scripture quotations are from the New Revised Standard Version of the Bible, are copyright © 1989 by the Division of Christian Education of the National Council of the Churches of Christ in the U.S.A, and are used by permission.

Scripture quotations marked RSV are from the Revised Standard Version of the Bible, copyright © 1946, 1952, 1971, and 1973 by the Division of Christian Education of the National Council of the Churches of Christ in the U.S.A., and are used by permission.

Book design by Sharon Adams
Cover design by Allison Taylor

Library of Congress Cataloging-in-Publication Data
Names: Long, Thomas G., 1946- honouree. I Johnston, Scott Black, editor. I
    Smith, Ted A., 1968- editor. I Tisdale, Leonora Tubbs, editor.
Title: Questions preachers ask : essays in honor of Thomas G. Long / Edited
    by Scott Black Johnston, Ted A. Smith, Leonora Tubbs Tisdale.
Description: First edition. I Louisville, KY : Westminster John Knox Press,
    2016. I Includes bibliographical references.
Identifiers: LCCN 2016006691 (print) I LCCN 2016016286 (ebook) I ISBN
    9780664261719 (alk. paper) I ISBN 9781611646900 (e-book)
Subjects: LCSH: Preaching.
Classification: LCC BV4222 .Q48 2016 (print) I LCC BV4222 (ebook) I DDC
    251--dc23
LC record available at https://lccn.loc.gov/2016006691

Most Westminster John Knox Press books are available at special quantity discounts when purchased in bulk by corporations, organizations, and special-interest groups. For more information, please e-mail SpecialSales@wjkbooks.com.

Contents

Foreword

CRAIG DYKSTRA

*T*his book is a Festschrift—a collection of writings that honor and celebrate the ministry of Thomas G. Long. One of the nation's finest preachers and one of the most influential and highly respected teachers of preaching in our time, Tom Long is a treasured gift who for more than forty years has shaped the ministries of thousands of seminary students and working pastors across this country and around the world. At least as peripatetic as the apostle Paul, he has preached and taught the gospel of Jesus Christ in countless congregations, colleges, universities, seminaries, and other assemblies. He has written more than a score of beautiful books and published hundreds of profoundly compelling sermons, essays, articles, and editorials, all of which proclaim the good news with great power. He has done all this with such depth and discernment—and with such a profound sense of what enables human beings to live the kind of life abundant to which God calls us—that those who hear and read him recognize immediately that they have encountered a witness who knows and tells the truth.

The chapters in this fine book are written by other outstanding preachers and teachers of preaching. Some of them have been Tom Long's students or colleagues. Others have known Tom over greater distances. All have reckoned with his work over many years. In this volume, the authors are each responding to a specific "question preachers ask." This is an entirely appropriate agenda for this particular Festschrift, since throughout his preaching and teaching ministry Tom Long has been addressing questions preachers ask—and, indeed, that a great many ordinary human beings ask—and responding to them insightfully and wisely. Indeed, Tom has special gifts for listening to all sorts of people's questions with uncommon care, for discerning what is really at stake in those questions, and for preaching sermons and writing books that speak to what matters most in those questions.

Tom Long knows every preacher's haunting nightmare, and he wrote about it on the first page of his first book:

> It is Sunday morning, the congregation settles into the pews after the final stanza of the sermon hymn, all eyes are on the pulpit, an air of electric quietness fills the sanctuary with anticipation . . . and the sermon is not finished. *yep!!*

Long knows the preacher's dread, the preacher's sense of inadequacy before her or his daunting task. But he also knows this:

> [that] sermons are *never* finished. There is always something else, something more, which can be said, should be said, but the time for preaching has arrived, and frail and incomplete thoughts must fill that deep cavern so innocently labeled "The Sermon." The broken labors of our hands and minds must now be trusted to the continuing sustenance of the Spirit and the faithful care of those who hear.[1]

Here we see, right at the start of his writing career, the gift that Tom Long both embodies and proclaims. It is the depth of his wisdom, born of knowing both what it means to be human (finite and fragile, scared halfway to death) and what it means to be loved by the triune God (upheld and sustained by ever-lasting forgiveness, grace, community, and love). As John Calvin wrote, "Nearly all the wisdom we possess, that is to say, true and sound wisdom, consists of two parts: the knowledge of God and of ourselves." This is the kind of wisdom we see in Tom Long.[2]

At the beginning of his classic text, *The Witness of Preaching*, Long poses the seemingly trivial but quite practical question that every preacher must somehow answer: How and through what door should the preacher enter the sanctuary? Long's response is to say that, logistically speaking, it doesn't matter much. But "if we look at this theologically," he writes, it matters greatly that worship leaders recognize that they "come from *within* the community of faith and not *to* it from the outside." Quoting Jürgen Moltmann, Long cements the point: "These people come from the community but come forward in front of it and act in Christ's name. It is not they as 'office bearers' who 'confront' the congregation; it is Christ. What they do and say is in the name of the triune God."[3] The whole rest of the book and Long's entire understanding of preaching is built on that conviction.

In his widely celebrated and extraordinarily influential book on the Christian funeral, Long poses the fundamental human question: What shall we do when someone dies? And then, more specifically, How shall we as Christians "care for, memorialize, and dispose of our dead"?[4] His answer runs long and deep into funeral practices in various cultures; the rich history of the theology and practice of the Christian funeral through the centuries; the cultural forces and attendant practices at play in contemporary America; and the significance of all of this for how pastors and preachers and people of faith may most richly embody the gospel in the church's own funeral practices. *Accompany Them with Singing* is both the title of the book and Long's rich answer to this very complex question: accompany them with singing . . . enacting the great, worshipful drama of the gospel . . . all along the way . . . all the way to the grave . . . in full cognizance of the promise of the good news of resurrection life.

Over and over again, in book after book and sermon after sermon, Tom Long takes up questions preachers ask—which in turn are almost always deeply connected to tough questions the people of and beyond their congregations are asking. "How can we worship faithfully and engagingly in the midst of rapid cultural change?" is the question Tom poses in *Beyond the Worship Wars*. Another book, *Preaching from Memory to Hope,* narrates a "bold and joyful approach to preaching" that is strong and vital enough to deal with what happens when "the trusted structures and strategies of the pulpit suddenly seem to lose their potency, and worried preachers, their confidence shaken, begin to scramble for the next, new thing."[5] *What Shall We Say?* is the title of a book in which Long addresses the question of how we as preachers can respond to profound questions regarding evil and suffering in the midst of a culture-wide crisis of faith.

Some years ago, I wrote an essay in which I said, "Somehow, pastors who really get what the Christian ministry is all about and who do it well are able to enter many diverse situations, whether joyous or full of misery and conflict, and see what is going on there through eyes of faith. This way of seeing and interpreting shapes what the pastor thinks and does and how he or she responds to people in gestures, words, and actions. It functions as a kind of internal gyroscope, guiding pastors in and through every crevice of pastoral life and work. This way of seeing and interpreting is [something I call] 'pastoral imagination.'"[6]

No one I know embodies a pastoral imagination more deeply, wisely, and well than Tom Long. In no small part, my understanding of this kind of imagination and this way of being a Christian minister, pastor, and preacher—a person responsible for fostering true, real, abundant life together in a community of faith—comes from knowing Tom Long. And we know each other very well. We have been closest friends for more than forty years. We first met in a seminar at Princeton Seminary, early in the time we were both doing doctoral studies. Our friendship bloomed immediately. Somehow we recognized in each other kindred spirits. Several years later, after teaching at different seminaries, we both returned to Princeton and taught there together for five wonderful years. We raised our kids together, played racquetball, taught our courses, served on faculty committees, and tried to dream up ways to shape theological education so that it could have its deepest and best impact on our students and the church. Since 1989, when I left Princeton to go to the Lilly Endowment, we have lived in different places. So for a long time, we haven't seen each other face-to-face nearly as often as we would like. But pretty much every week we talk on the phone, usually for an hour, to tell each other what's on our minds and to discuss the church, the ministry, theology, politics, social issues, books, music, baseball, our children and grandchildren—in sum, our lives. We talk on the phone in order to keep one another company on this sacred journey along the way.

I am grateful for the wonderful, deep friendship Tom and I have shared—and will continue to share for as long as we both are living. And I am glad for this volume that honors Tom, that displays the influence he has had on many of today's leading teachers of preaching, and that extends his legacy by taking up some very important and challenging "questions preachers ask." I expect that as you read this book, you will note resonances with both the substance and the manner in which Tom Long pursued his craft. You will no doubt also perceive significant departures and differences—perhaps even serious arguments. That will be fine with Tom. Part of his genius, part of his gift, has been to teach and to preach in such a way that each person whom he taught and to whom he preached would ask and address the questions at hand themselves—in their own ways, bringing their own particular gifts to bear—so that the voices of the whole, wide, diverse, God-blessed, and beautiful church might sing in a chorus of praise to the one God who is the ultimate giver and sustainer of life in every time and place.

Read this book. Then go back and read (or reread) some of Tom Long's books as well. Your ministry and your life will be enriched and renewed.

Acknowledgments

We are grateful for the many people who helped make this volume possible. The preachers who responded to our initial requests provided questions of insight and integrity that set the stage for the whole book. All the busy contributors made time to write excellent essays on topics that they did not get to choose. David Dobson of Westminster John Knox, Jan Love of Candler School of Theology, and Kimberly Long of Columbia Theological Seminary each provided important support for the project. And Hyemin Na of Emory University helped prepare the final manuscript with extraordinary intelligence and attention to detail.

This book was prepared to honor Thomas G. Long on the occasion of his retirement from full-time teaching at Emory's Candler School of Theology. And while he was not directly involved in the production of this book, it is safe to say that no one contributed more. His ideas are our steady conversation partners through the book. And his teaching, mentorship, and friendship helped form the editors and authors. This book is dedicated to him with thanks to God.

Advent 2015

Scott Black Johnston
Fifth Avenue Presbyterian Church, New York

Ted A. Smith
Candler School of Theology, Emory University

Leonora Tubbs Tisdale
Yale Divinity School

Introduction

SCOTT BLACK JOHNSTON, TED A. SMITH,
AND LEONORA TUBBS TISDALE

*T*his book began as a labor of love to honor the many contributions Thomas G. Long has made to the church, the academy, and wider society. Two of its editors (Scott Black Johnston and Nora Tubbs Tisdale) were Tom Long's doctoral students at Princeton Theological Seminary and experienced his wise mentorship, teaching, and guidance through that formative process. Two of us (Ted Smith at Candler School of Theology and Nora Tisdale while at Princeton Theological Seminary) have been faculty colleagues of Long and have had the privilege of teaching in this field with him, often using his books as our textbooks. One of us (Scott Black Johnston) is both a former professor of preaching and the current pastor of a large New York City congregation (Fifth Avenue Presbyterian Church) where Long serves frequently as a guest preacher. All three of us have considered Tom Long a treasured friend, a valued mentor, and a fellow pilgrim in the life of faith and service to God and to the church.

When we first began talking several years ago about what kind of book we should craft in Long's honor, we considered a number of possibilities. We talked about a book in biblical hermeneutics, given Long's deep interest in Scripture and its interpretation in preaching. We considered a book on the form of the sermon, a topic on which we three have learned especially from Long. The possibilities kept expanding as we thought through his different works. After all, he has written books of enduring significance on topics as diverse as what makes for a good funeral, the crises of faith that can come with suffering, the ways that the literary forms of the Bible should influence the shaping of sermons, the meaning and value of faithful testimony in daily life, the rise of Gnosticism in contemporary spirituality, and the importance of preaching eschatological hope in a time of cynicism and despair. Given the range and depth of the questions Long has addressed, we had no shortage of topics that might orient a Festschrift!

After considerable discussion, we finally decided we should start this book where the books of Long himself so often begin: with the questions preachers are actually asking. Time after time, in both his books and his articles, Long has identified cutting-edge issues pastors and faith communities are facing and then tackled them with biblical and theological depth, intellectual acumen, and pastoral sensitivity. While he has written on many topics, and across many genres, this ability to connect with the questions of preachers and other people of faith runs through all of his work. This deep connection to the lived stuff of faith is all the more remarkable given his long service and high attainments in academic settings. Long's work spans church and academy in ways that have become increasingly rare—and all the more important.

Rather than beginning this book with our own preconceived notions regarding what preachers "need," we decided to ask some preachers we admire what questions are most pressing for them about preaching and its practice. In the summer of 2013 we polled a group of about thirty North American preachers, consulting some by e-mail, some by phone, and some in person. The preachers we polled serve in contexts that are diverse in terms of denomination, race, ethnicity, geography, size, and institutional shape. Our sample was not large enough or random enough to support sweeping sociological claims about what is on the minds of preachers in North America. But that was not our purpose. Our purpose was to listen carefully to some wise people who could help us connect the book more organically to the living concerns of at least some preachers today.

We asked each preacher to respond to two questions:

1. What are the most significant challenges that you are facing regarding the task of preaching in your particular context?
2. What questions is the present cultural moment raising for you about the task of preaching?

In response to these questions we received a batch of extraordinarily thoughtful responses. We compiled the responses and distilled them into a list of eleven questions. These questions provided the starting points for the chapters of this book. Some of the questions that frame the chapters are verbatim restatements of questions we received from preachers. Others are composites that we created by attending to concerns shared by multiple respondents. We then recruited a group of pastoral scholars and scholarly pastors who had the gifts and expertise to address the questions these preachers were asking. Not coincidentally, the gifts and expertise demanded by these questions were found in unusual concentrations among the friends and former students of Tom Long.

Craig Dykstra writes the foreword that frames the book not just because he is one of Long's closest friends, but because his own work on the importance of Christian practices has done so much to shape the context in which a book like this can even be conceived. Dykstra's foreword rightly turns the book toward pastors, not only as people to be addressed, but also as sources of the kind of insight and imagination that drive the best theology.

And what are the questions preachers today are asking? As the structure of this book indicates, they are varied.

Some questions have to do with *the changing role of the Bible* in today's church and society. How do we preach to people who have little grounding in the Bible and little knowledge of the "old, old story" that people of faith hold dear (ch. 1)? Are there particular genres of biblical literature that can speak with particular power to contemporary people (ch. 2)? Are there ways to structure preaching over the course of a year or a lifetime so that preachers from lectionary-based traditions can honor the lectionary without being enslaved to it (ch. 3)?

Other questions acknowledge the *theological and religious pluralism* of our age. How do we preach in a way that affirms Christian theology while honoring the insights of other faith traditions (ch. 4)? How do we understand the "authority" of the preacher in an age in which concepts of authority are ever-shifting (ch. 5)?

Another set of questions addresses the *changing congregational contexts* for contemporary preaching. How do we preach to faith communities that are highly diverse in terms of race, ethnicity, class, theological background, sexual orientation, and more (ch. 6)? How do we proclaim good news to young adults who are on the margins of church or have left it (ch. 7)? How do we preach to communities within the church that are increasingly depressed and discouraged because of the loss of "church" as it once was (ch. 8)?

A *changing society and culture* also present challenges for contemporary preaching. How do we preach effectively to a people who are used to sound bites, Twitter feeds, and a visual entertainment culture? How do we create genuine Christian community in an age of social networking (ch. 9)? How do we preach prophetically in a time of deep divisions without being ignored (ch. 10)?

Finally, contemporary preachers are looking for *signs of hope* for preaching. It is easy enough to name some places where preachers are struggling. But worrying that preaching has lost its way is one of the most enduring tropes in the history of the church in the United States. And this worry is often raised right at the time that new life is already breaking forth just out of sight of the one who is raising it. And so we wanted to close with preachers' questions about signs of hope on the landscape of preaching today. What can we learn about preaching from the new things the Holy Spirit is already doing in our midst (ch. 11)?

Following a venerable sermon style, the book ends with a poem. This triptych comes from Long's friend and collaborator Thomas Lynch. Lynch follows the preacher into the hard questions raised by the sayings of Jesus. "So," he writes, "what shall we say to these things? Who's to know?" Lynch then offers answers to these preachers' questions:

> Say God is love. Love God. Love one another.
> Say grace is undeserved and plentiful.
> Say if we're saved, it's mostly from ourselves.

Amen. The questions of preachers might not allow for easy answers. But they can call forth poetry.

We do not pretend that this list of questions about preaching is exhaustive. Nor do we assume that the answers offered are the last word on these topics. What we hope this book will do is facilitate and deepen conversations around some of the critical questions of our day. And we are deeply grateful to the stellar group of people who contributed to this book. We appreciate the wisdom, faith, and intellect they bring to the process of considering these questions. We appreciate their gifts for practical theology that lives up to the full promise of that phrase.

Tom Long helped set the course these chapters follow, for he has contributed on multiple levels to the flourishing of practical theology. In the preface to the third edition of his homiletics textbook *The Witness of Preaching*—a book that has been used in countless classrooms around the world—Long names an important change in practical theology:

> As the first edition of this book was being written . . . a sea change was taking place in the understanding of practical theology, including homiletics. Instead of thinking of practical theology as merely applied theology, practical theology was beginning to emerge as a generative theological discipline in its own right. The actual lived experience of faithful people—as individuals, in churches and other communities, through their religious rituals and practices, and in their engagement with society—was increasingly being seen as a *source* for theological knowledge and not just as a *target*, the place toward which one shot doctrinal arrows sharpened somewhere else. We began to recognize that the ways the church preached over its history,

as well as the ways it celebrated the Lord's Supper or showed hospitality to the stranger, were not just applied theology; they *were* theology—lived theology, theology in action, theology embedded in practice. So, practical theologians, instead of simply packaging and retailing formal theology for the mass market or giving helps and hints for surefire results in the church, now understood themselves to be directing traffic in the middle of a busy three-way intersection, with knowledge coursing back and forth among dogmatics, the practices of the church, and "secular" disciplines, each with its claims and effects on the other.

As a result of this new understanding of practical theology, Long wrote, "homiletics began gradually to develop a highly creative and theoretically sophisticated literature."[1] Long was not just describing this transformation. He was helping to lead it. And he continues to provide leadership now through his work as a scholar, a teacher of preachers, a teacher of teachers of preachers, and a preacher himself.

For over four decades Tom Long has stood at the intersection of the Bible, theology, church practice, and related secular disciplines, crafting practical theology from and for preaching. He is the author of practical theological works that are highly creative, deeply insightful, and theologically sophisticated. In his teaching, writing, and preaching he has made an impact on countless pastors, laypeople, scholars, and teachers of preaching. Our hope is that this volume—which begins with the practices of preachers, takes seriously the insights of preachers, and wrestles with the questions preachers ask—will not only honor but also continue that legacy.

PART I   Bible

Chapter 1

Shaped by Hearing

Living Our Stories Together

GAIL R. O'DAY[1]

How do we reclaim the Bible in the pulpit for people who have little grounding in it or connection to it?

The opportunity to write an essay on the occasion of Thomas G. Long's retirement from the Candler School of Theology faculty brings back rich and happy memories of team-teaching with Professor Long in the introductory preaching course at Candler, helping prepare students for their preaching ministries. A volume of essays that derives its themes from the questions of preachers who have active preaching ministries is an appropriate way to mark the teaching career of a person who has always had his mind and heart on the sacred vocation of those who preach every week.

Reclaim or Proclaim?

One of the preachers surveyed asked a question that distilled the concerns of many others: "How do we reclaim the Bible in the pulpit for people who have little grounding in it or connection to it?" This question leads me to ask a series of questions in reply: What moment in the life of the church and what model of congregational biblical literacy constitute the gold standard against which today's congregations are found lacking? What understanding of the preacher and the sermon's relationship to the Bible does this question assume? And does this essay's framing question inadvertently establish a hierarchy of listeners, with those who "know" the Bible in a different classification than those who "have little grounding in it or connection to it"?

The framing question reflects religious leaders' anxiety about the level of "biblical literacy" among congregations that is fed and exacerbated by mass media reports that highlight the decline in church membership and the

3

growth in the percentage of those who claim no formal religious affiliation. Against the background noise of such media chatter, a pastoral leader has to work hard to avoid succumbing to the trap that the reporting on such studies sets: to accept the premise that our current age is indeed an age of decline for the work of the gospel. Such a general premise can become a worldview that sees decline in every kind of change. It can give an all-encompassing narrative shape to what may actually be discrete observations, underwriting a story in which people know less about the Bible than they did in "the good old days." That story becomes a real trap when preachers assume that the effectiveness of the proclamation of God's good news for the world hinges on the knowledge of the Bible that congregants bring with them to worship.

A second potential trap is related to this first one. To posit that a significant role of the preacher is to reclaim the Bible in the pulpit assumes an extrinsic authority of scripture that the preacher must convey to a worshipping congregation. The pastoral contribution of preaching to the life of a worshipping community and the creative power of the individual preacher are severely constrained and limited by the assumption that a preacher cannot preach effectively if the congregation does not come to worship with "grounding" in or prior connection to the Bible. Understood this way, preaching risks becoming primarily a transactional act of communication through which the preacher gives something to the congregation, and what the preacher has to give can be received only if the congregation already knows something about what the preacher is giving them. In this understanding of preaching, the sermon reinforces preexisting and commonly held assumptions about content and sources of authority, and the congregation gathers to be reminded by the preacher of what they should already know about the Bible, a decidedly passive role for the hearers of the word.

Yet perhaps ironically, the transactional model of preaching that echoes in the background of this question also creates a passive role for the preacher. The language of reclaiming is language that assumes that there is something that exists in an objectively verifiable moment or place that has been lost and needs to be found. The image of the Bible sitting in the lost-and-found pile, waiting for the preacher to reclaim it, is hard to resist. If the preacher is relegated to the role of "reclaiming" the Bible in the pulpit, however, where does the preacher's authority to "claim" or "proclaim" reside?[2] In the transactional model of communication, the power of scripture for preaching depends on congregational pre-knowledge of its content, and the preacher is relegated to the role of reclaimer, not proclaimer, suggesting that little if anything is actually created in and through preaching.

The pastoral vocation and its preaching ministry are demanding enough without the additional limitations that this understanding of the Bible and preaching imposes on the preacher. This essay will propose an alternative way to envision the relationship between Bible and sermon that frees, rather than constrains, the preacher for the proclamation of God's good news.

The Bible and the Worshipper

A quick review of the way in which worshippers have engaged the Bible throughout Christian history reveals the historical and ecclesial shortsightedness of the notion that the efficacy of preaching depends on the level of biblical literacy and prior biblical connection of those who gather for worship. The textual history of the Bible is a reminder that individual tangible copies of the contents of the Bible, whether written on parchment or papyrus, in scroll or codex form, were scarce commodities in the ancient world.[3] Private ownership of a copy of the Bible was rare in the early centuries of the church, as the means of producing copies required more money and technical proficiency than most individuals had at their disposal. Sacred texts, both Jewish and Christian, were copied by hand by paid professionals at a scriptorium or by scribes in various religious and monastic communities. The written word has always been revered in Christianity; the English language names for Christianity's sacred texts reflect this reverence. "Scripture" is a transliteration of the Latin for "that which is written," and "Bible" is a transliteration of the Greek for "books." Yet for most Christians living outside the monasteries in the first centuries of the church, the revered written word was accessed through hearing the word in community, not through private study and personal devotion.

This pattern continued for centuries. For much of Jewish and Christian history, the revered written word was not available for most communities in their vernacular language. The classic Hebrew of much of the Hebrew scriptures was not spoken in the Greco-Roman world in which synagogue worship took root—as evidenced by Aramaic targums (translation and interpretations of the Hebrew into the Aramaic vernacular, rendered originally during a public reading of scripture in worship) and the LXX (Septuagint) translation of the Hebrew scriptures into Greek. Later, as the Roman Empire grew and consolidated its power, both secular and religious, scriptures were translated into Latin. And yet each Latin translation—the Old Latin, Jerome's Latin translation, the Vulgate—still was for public reading, hearing, and instruction. As the Roman empire faded and the vernacular languages and governments of Western and Eastern Europe and Asia Minor emerged, vernacular translations began to appear—again for public reading, not private devotion. And because these early translations and versions were hand copied, not printed, a Bible for every home or a Bible for every believer was not understood as a necessary condition for "knowing" and being connected to scripture.

For the majority of centuries of Christian preaching and worship, then, grounding in scripture was primarily a liturgical experience in which scripture was experienced and known through public reading, public interpretation, and the liturgies of the church. The extant sermons of John Chrysostom and Augustine, for example, show how these renowned early preachers often proceeded through a continuous reading of a biblical book with a series of sermons. Such procession did not depend on their hearers' knowing the texts in advance. The act of preaching itself brought the worshipping community into the biblical story in an active and transformative way. The difference is not just when the congregation came to know the Bible, but how.

Prevailing modern conceptions of biblical knowledge tend to focus on mastery of the Bible as a book of facts. Knowing the Bible involves the kind of knowledge that might be attained through a school-like study apart from worship. But careful examination of monastic reading practices from earlier centuries reveals that Christian communities valued different ways of knowing the Bible—ways that could be gained only in experiences of worship in community. Worship in these communities did not depend on prior knowledge of the Bible. Worship enabled all those gathered—including the preacher—to come to know the Bible in the ways that reshaped their imaginations and their understanding of God in the world.[4]

The shift to each individual reading her or his own Bible can be traced directly to the advent of movable type with Johannes Gutenberg in the middle years of the fifteenth century. Movable type began to make possible the mass production of Bibles. If movable type made it possible for more people to own Bibles, translation was required for more people to be able to read the Bibles they could now own. Reformation leaders like Martin Luther, John Calvin, William Tyndale, and Myles Coverdale all shared in the project of translation. Simply creating a vernacular translation was not in and of itself a revolutionary form of protest. Vernacular translations of scripture predated the time of Jesus, as noted above. What made the translation battles revolutionary was the way movable type encouraged and made possible claims of *sola scriptura* and the practice of private Bible reading. Because the individual Christian was no longer dependent on the communal worship gathering for his or her access to scripture, this new technology changed the very epistemology of reading and engaging the Bible. The Bible became something the individual could now read in private, instead of hearing aloud as an act of communal formation.

Twenty-first-century preachers ignore this history to our peril, because more of the history and life of the Christian worshipping community existed (and thrived) before the invention of the printing press than after. A way forward is to contemplate what we have given up through an unquestioning acceptance of a notion of biblical literacy based on the technology of the printing press and a norm of private Bible study as the only meaningful measure of what it means to be grounded in the Bible. A way forward is to ponder what preaching may have lost—and what it could possibly reclaim—if we moved the defining locus for "knowing" the Bible away from private devotion and study and located it instead in the Bible's generative power in communal worship.

Faith and Hearing

The New Testament itself reminds us of the communal nature of biblical "literacy." Luke 4:14–30, the first act of Jesus' public ministry in Luke, depicts scripture reading and its public interpretation in the first-century synagogue, the worship practice out of which early Christian worship grew. Verses 16–20 show Jesus in the role of lector and narrate in vivid detail the practices of reading that prevailed in the synagogue at that time. The text depicts Jesus unrolling the scroll, finding and reading the assigned Isaiah text for the day, and rerolling the scroll, all with a scroll attendant standing by. Verse 20 underscores this public, liturgical context, taking care to note that "the eyes of all in the synagogue were fixed upon him." The public reading and communal hearing of the written sacred word created expectancy in those who heard. And because the story is narrated in something close to real time for those who hear this Gospel story read to them, those hearers become de facto members of the synagogue community. Verses 21–30 portray Jesus in the role of interpreter of the written sacred word. The words with which Jesus begins his interpretation, "Today this scripture is fulfilled in your hearing" (v. 21), focus the synagogue hearers in the story and those who hear the Lukan story on the centrality of this particular moment of communal hearing in claiming the power of scripture for the worshipping community. The two worshipping communities are overlaid in a brilliant narrative move—those who hear Luke read out loud can also imagine themselves in the synagogue with Jesus as he reads aloud.

The four key elements of Luke 4:21—today / this scripture/ is fulfilled / in your (second person plural) hearing—are a poignant reminder that communal worship is not about reclaiming the Bible but about the holy possibility of hearing the Bible together for the first time. Jesus does not say that fulfillment happened in some past act of study, "in your confirmation class, in last week's Bible study, in your morning devotional," but today, in this moment, right now. He does not ask them to remember something from the past about the scripture but instead says that in this very moment as they gather together, the scripture is fulfilled. Nor does he say "the scriptures" as a totality ("the writings") are fulfilled. It is rather "this scripture" ("*this* writing"), *hē graphē hautē*—the scripture just read and heard—that is fulfilled. Fulfillment happens as the scripture is read aloud in the corporate act of worship.

These four elements provide a way forward for today's preacher to recognize and embrace the transformative power of the Bible and preaching because they name what can happen only in the shared moment of hearing scripture together in worship: (a) the immediacy of each worship moment ("today"); (b) the shared hearing of a biblical text ("this scripture") that creates its own mode of "knowing" the Bible; (c) the preacher's articulated conviction about the power of transformation within the communal encounter with scripture ("is fulfilled"); and (d) the active role of the congregation's gathered presence in worship ("in your hearing"). Luke 4:21 offers an imaginatively engaging alternative to contemporary malaise and complaining refrains about biblical literacy today, because it shows us that what worshippers bring from the Bible to worship pales beside what the Bible can bring to the gathered community. The Bible is not a story of the past that needs to be reclaimed in the pulpit but a story of the present and future that needs to be proclaimed in the pulpit.

 This theme resounds throughout the Bible: it is not what one knows about the Bible before hearing it proclaimed that is transformative; it is what one hears as a biblical text is proclaimed that is transformative. On this point, perhaps we preachers need to question our own biblical literacy! For example, Paul recalls the Galatians to the origins of their faith journey by saying to them, "It was before your eyes that Jesus Christ was publicly displayed as crucified" (Gal. 3:1). How did this public display occur other than through Paul's proclamation of the story? This was not a story they had known previously but a story that became real to them in Paul's proclamation of it. And in a revealing rhetorical choice, the Greek word that Paul uses to talk about this public display is *proegraphē*, literally, "written before your eyes," so that Paul is equating the impact of hearing with that of seeing a publicly displayed placard. Proclaiming and hearing has the same impact as writing and reading—so that again, concern about prior literacy skews the conversation about preaching. The "literacy" that public proclamation creates is what matters for faith.

Paul expresses the same conviction of the efficacy and necessity of proclamation in Romans 10:14: "And how are they to believe in one of whom they have never heard? And how are they to hear without someone who proclaims?" He names the conviction that sustains these questions in 10:17, writing, "Therefore faith is from hearing." Paul's passionate conviction about the power of proclamation was shaped in an age when there could only be one source of biblical "literacy": the proclaimer whose spoken words could write the stories of faith before the gathered community's eyes. Have we preachers allowed ourselves to lose this conviction about the generative and transformative power of proclamation because of the ready access to printed Bibles and to a seemingly endless array of translations marketed for every kind of demographic group? Has our governing assumption shifted from "faith is from hearing" to "faith is from the level of biblical literacy that you attained in study before worship"?

Rowan Williams provides a helpful perspective on this question in his recent book, *Being Christian: Baptism, Bible, Eucharist, Prayer.* The title of the book names what Williams takes to be the essential elements of Christian life. Williams begins his chapter on the Bible with this reminder:

> [F]or the huge majority of Christians throughout the centuries, as well as for many today, the Bible is a book *heard* more than read. And that is quite a significant fact about it. For when you see a group of baptized people listening to the Bible in public worship, you realize that Bible-reading is an essential part of Christian life because *Christian life is a listening life.* Christians are people who expect to be spoken to by God.[5]

The enervating worldview alluded to at the beginning of this essay, in which every change is read as a narrative of decline, may have blocked preachers' access to this seemingly simple experience named by Rowan Williams. Communal hearing creates something that did not and could not exist prior to that moment of shared listening. How many preachers fall into the trap of thinking every sermon needs to say something new—even on Easter Sunday, when there is only one thing to say and one thing that needs to be heard, "Christ is risen." Preachers are invited to realize that each moment of proclamation is by definition something new, something that did not exist until these gathered people shared together in this moment of hearing the presence of God spoken out loud among them.

Reclaiming the Power and Possibility of Proclamation

As an imaginative exercise, let us as preachers start our conversation about Bible and preaching from the transformative and creative possibility of the moment of communal speaking and hearing and not from the point of the inadequate formation and preparation of those who gather eager to hear. Let us as preachers align ourselves with everyone who comes to worship—newcomers, weekly regulars, Sunday School teachers, visitors formed (or not!) in other traditions, and more—and with them enter into the preaching moment with the expectancy that God's offer of new life will be heard through our proclamation of this Sunday's particular glimpse of the story of God in the world.

I still know of no one who names this possibility more poignantly and hopefully than Lutheran theologian and preacher Joseph Sittler:

> In a sense, that's what a sermon is for: to hang the holy possible in front of the mind of the listeners and lead them to that wonderful moment when they say, "If that were true, it would do." To pass from that to belief is the work of the Holy Spirit, not of the preacher or the teacher.[6]

The proclaimer's privilege and responsibility is not to reclaim an old story but to proclaim with confidence in a way that "hangs the holy possible" before a congregation. Preaching does not revolve around biblical knowledge; it revolves around biblical imagination, and a worshipping congregation needs the preacher to believe that this is possible—that proclamation can evoke for the listening community a glimpse of life with God that did not exist before that moment of communal engagement with the proclaimed word. The preacher is not reminding with words; the preacher is creating with words. Or, to put it in even more biblically evocative language: the preacher is cocreating with God, because the range of Christian tradition and texts invites the preacher to trust and embrace the power of words to create new realities:

> Then God said, "Let there be light" . . . (Gen. 1:3)

> In the beginning was the Word, and the Word was with God, and the Word was God (John 1:1)[7]

The God of biblical tradition is one who creates through speaking. The Genesis 1 creation account does not depict God "making" but God speaking, and through God's words, newness is birthed. John reminds his readers of the generative power of God's word when he frames his Gospel as another story of the generative word.

It matters little how much pre-knowledge of the Bible individual members of a worshipping community bring with them into any gathering. It matters much that preachers accept the invitation that the God of the Bible offers us—to embrace the creative power of the word through which we were first called into being and which can continue to call us into being—and to let that power and possibility resound in our proclamation.

Sittler's sense of "the holy possible" helps to focus on why and how the framing question for this essay misplaces the burden of responsibility for the preacher and for the listening community. The question that launched this essay focuses on what isn't possible, while Sittler's powerful insight assumes unequivocally what is not just possible but promised. The preacher's responsibility is to trust the generative power of the shared experience of proclamation and so to make the "old" story today's story, with the same conviction articulated by Paul and enacted by Jesus in the Nazareth synagogue. This act of cocreation does not hinge on prior biblical literacy but on the preacher trusting that his or her words can draw deep on God's creating words and summon a new creation into the imagination of those gathered to listen.

Proclaiming, not reclaiming, is the preacher's vocation. Or to use a chapter heading from one of Professor Long's books, "no news is bad news."[8] This nice turn on gospel as "good news" underscores an important point—something new happens in a sermon, something that has not been said before is said with these people on this day, and if we let go of the act of proclaiming the news that is created in this moment and focus instead on reclamation, then we are left with no news.

Blessed Are Those Who Have Not Seen and Yet Believe

To focus on preaching as an act of cocreation, as the proclamation of the "holy possible," instead of as the reclaiming and reminding of a set of stories and teachings that the congregation ought to know already, is crucial for the communal transformation that undergirds a preaching ministry. Because when we focus on proclamation, on what happens with this word in this moment with and for these people, then no one hearer is privileged over another. The disciples who were in the room when Jesus appeared to them after the resurrection are no more blessed than Thomas, who happened to be absent at that time (John 20:19–29), nor are they more blessed than later generations of believers who also were not in that room (John 20:29).

When we understand preaching as proclamation instead of reclamation, we live into the conviction that all members of the gathered community, the preacher included, are equal, that all are one, in the same moment, in the same hope of transformative possibility, in the same delight in the surprise of the gospel.

Chapter 2

Form Follows Function

Well-Shaped Sermons for the Twenty-First Century

ALYCE M. McKENZIE

What do we do with all the different kinds of literature that are in the Bible?

Are there particular genres and forms—both biblical and sermonic—that can speak to contemporary people with particular power?

*O*n the way out the door at the end of a worship service, people comment on the sermon as they shake the preacher's hand. The most common remarks are general and positive. Frequently heard comments include "Nice sermon," "Enjoyed your sermon," and "Good job." Sometimes comments focus a bit more specifically on the sermon's content. "You gave us a lot to think about," people say. "The story you told at the end was very moving."

Only every now and then does someone make a comment that relates to the form of the sermon. "You really held my attention," someone might say, or, "I appreciate the way you connect the Bible and life in your sermons."

And no one, in all my years of preaching, has ever come out of a service, shaken my hand, and said, "I really admire your form, pastor." For one thing, it sounds slightly inappropriate. For another, most listeners are not equipped to listen for and analyze the form of our sermons. Who is going to say, "I appreciated the way you began with a sharp hook that revealed our investment in the issue and then connected it by means of an apt analogy to the text and then alternated between the world of the text and the world of today"? Maybe a high school English teacher, a professor of rhetoric at a local college, or a retired pastor. Maybe. But probably not. It's not the congregation's job to analyze the form of our sermons. Shaping a coherent and compelling sermon form is *our* job as preachers. And it's more important now than ever before.

In 1989 I applied to the PhD program in Practical Theology at Princeton

Theological Seminary to study homiletics. I still remember my elation at receiving my letter of acceptance and, a few days later, a personal letter of welcome from Dr. Thomas G. Long. He became the advisor for my PhD dissertation, a trusted mentor, and, in the years since I graduated, a colleague and friend. Much of what I have learned about writing, preaching, and teaching I have learned from him. In particular, much of what I have learned about sermon form, the focus of this essay, I owe to him. And I am by no means the only one!

In his books, articles, teaching, and preaching, Long is like a master jeweler who lifts up the notion of form and turns it so that light refracts through its various facets. In *The Witness of Preaching,* Long considers the facet of the identity of the preacher and his or her understanding of the purpose of preaching. In *Preaching and the Literary Forms of the Bible,* Long turns to a different aspect of form, considering the literary genre of the biblical text on which the sermon is based. And in a series of essays and articles, Long explores form once more, shedding light on the preacher's cultural context. In considering the topic of form from so many different angles, Long helps us understand the nature and significance of this homiletical gem.

A Profound Respect for Form

Long's work is based on a profound respect for what he calls "the formfulness of human communication." Says Long, "Whenever people communicate with each other, they do more than employ words and gestures. They place those verbal and nonverbal elements into some kind of recognizable pattern, that is, into a form." Long contends that we speak and listen according to certain formal patterns as members of a language community.[1] The particular language community in which preaching occurs is the church, "the speech community of God."[2] Long is attentive to the form of our testimony both within the church and beyond its walls as we put "our faith into words out in streets and avenues of daily life."[3] This focus on form weaves its way through the broad spectrum of his writings. His work is characterized by a respect for the narrative scope and shape of our Christian witness in preaching and worship.

In *Beyond the Worship Wars* (2001), one of the nine features of faithful worship Long cites is a recovery of the sense of drama inherent in Christian worship. This is a comment about form. The pattern of conflict and resolution that makes for drama is the key dynamic of narrative. It provides that forward moving propulsion we call plot. And worship, Long argues, should follow the plot of the saving story of creation: fall, redemption, and new creation.

In *Preaching from Memory to Hope* (2009), Long laments the fact that we have truncated that plot and all but excised the ending of our Christian story. A restoration of consciousness of the end times of judgment and return might not help people peer into the future, Long writes, but it would help us view the present in light of hope. At its heart, Long's lament in this book is about the *form* of our witness.

In *Accompany Them with Singing* (2009) and *The Good Funeral: Death, Grief, and the Community of Care* (2013), Long identifies the biblical, theological, and liturgical shortcomings of much contemporary Christian funeral practice. They compress a play of several acts into a single scene that all but ignores the body. The preparation, presence, and committal of the body all disappear in thin "celebrations of life." The sacred identity of the deceased is underemphasized, and the participation of the mourners is shortchanged. Among other things, this is a problem with the *form* of the funeral liturgy.

Again and again, across countless texts and topics, the broad sweep of Long's writing shows his profound concern for form in both preaching and worship. Every century has, of course, had its forms of choice, but the 1970s brought a self-awareness about form's role and importance, a willingness to critique the assumptions about the forms of past centuries.

A Critique of Traditional Sermon Form

In the early 1970s there was a marked shift in the favored homiletical form used by North American preachers in mainline Protestant denominations. The shift was from deductive, three-point preaching to inductive, narrative preaching. With this transition the clearest statement of the preacher's theme moved from the beginning of the sermon to the end. Preachers replaced evidence and explanation with a process of discovery.

Jumpstarted by the publication of Fred Craddock's *As One without Authority* in 1971, homiletician Eugene Lowry baptized this shift as a "Revolution in Sermonic Shape." It came to be called "The New Homiletic." It sprang from a critique of the form of traditional, deductive preaching and the assumption on which that preaching was based: that the preacher and the conceptual content of the sermon are the primary sources of authority and meaning in preaching. Others voices joined Craddock's in lifting up the deficiencies in the form of traditional preaching. "Where is your plot?" asked Eugene Lowry, jazz musician and then professor of preaching at St. Paul School of Theology in Kansas City. "Where is your imaginative language?" asked Charles Rice, Professor of Homiletics at Drew Theological School, Drew University, as he recommended that preachers learn from novelists and short story writers. David Buttrick, who taught homiletics and liturgics at Vanderbilt University Divinity School, asked, "Where are your moves?" and set forth a specific, strategic approach to sermon form in his *Homiletic: Moves and Structures.* Henry Mitchell, Professor of Homiletics at the Interdenominational Theological Center in Atlanta, Georgia, asked, "Where is your celebration?" All these challenges to traditional preaching criticized it for its neglect of form and recommended renewed respect for form moving forward.

But Why Is Form Important in the First Place?

By the late 1980s, with the narrative, inductive approach to preaching in full force, there was plenty being written about why traditional forms were no longer compelling. We needed someone to step back from the fray and offer a clear-eyed assessment of why form is important in the first place, what it has to do with the meaning and impact of a sermon. It was at that point, in 1989, that Tom Long published *The Witness of Preaching,* a clear, cogent introductory preaching text that has enjoyed several printings and that is widely used in seminary preaching classes. The book is one whose significance continues to unfold after graduation; it holds pride of place on many preachers' bookshelves. And at the center of *Witness* is a statement about the crucial role of sermon form: "Despite the fact that it passes by relatively unnoticed, form is absolutely vital to the meaning and effect of a sermon. Like the silent shifting of gears in a car's automatic transmission, sermon form translates the potential energy of the sermon into productive movement, while remaining itself quietly out of view."[4] Long continues with an explanation of why form matters so much:

> Instead of thinking of sermon form and content as separate realities, . . . it is far better to speak of the *form of the content.* A sermon's form, although often largely unperceived by the hearers, provides shape and energy to the sermon and thus becomes itself a vital force in how a sermon makes meaning. . . . In the simplest of terms, a sermon form is an organizational plan for deciding what kinds of things will be said and done in a sermon and in what sequence.[5]

Long quotes Halford E. Luccock's view of the crucial role of sermon form as stated in his 1944 preaching textbook *In the Minister's Workshop:* "The power of a sermon lies in its structure, not in its decoration. Form is as important to the flow and direction of a sermon as are the banks of a river to the movement of its currents."[6]

Form Follows Function:
The Identity of the Preacher Shapes the Form of the Sermon

The American architect Louis Sullivan wrote an article in 1896 titled "The Tall Office Building Artistically Considered" in which he made the statement that "form ever follows function." In the late 1800s in Chicago, Sullivan developed the shape of the tall steel skyscraper. It was a time of economic and technological innovation. Established styles no longer accommodated contemporary needs. If the shape of the building was not going to be chosen out of the old pattern book, something else had to determine form. According to Sullivan, that something was going to be the purpose of the building. For Sullivan and those who looked to him for guidance, "form follows precedent" gave way to "form follows function."

The Witness of Preaching demonstrates that what is true in architecture can be true in preaching as well: form follows function. The way preachers view their purpose in preaching determines the form they favor in their sermons from week to week. Long identifies four models for the identity of the preacher and the corresponding way she or he understands the purpose of preaching: the herald, the storyteller, the pastor, and the witness. Each of these models of identity has implications for the form of the sermon.

If a preacher sees herself as a herald, focused on the biblical, theological message without particular concern for rhetorical shaping or congregational exegesis, she may be drawn toward the deductive, three-point-sermon form. The potential pitfall is that sermons may be predictable and focused on the intellect to the neglect of emotion and imagination. If the preacher sees himself as a storyteller, he may be drawn to an inductive, narrative form of preaching. The risk here is that the larger theological and biblical themes may get lost in the details of the stories, and the sermon's ethical impact may be missing in action. If a preacher sees herself primarily as a pastor, she will likely be drawn to forms that stress divine solutions to human problems. This form becomes problematic if it implies that God exists primarily to solve our problems and that discipleship makes our lives simpler and more manageable.

People are not sitting in the pews asking themselves as we preach, "I wonder which model of the identity of the preacher she is going by and how that is shaping her sense of the purpose and form of her sermon?" But again even casual comments at the door reveal how they have experienced us and the impact of our messages. "You really gave us something to think about and you really stepped on some toes" suggests that they heard the preacher as a herald. "I felt you were speaking just to me and my problems" points to an experience of the preacher as pastor. "The story you told reminded me of something that happened to me" continues the conversation begun by a preacher heard as a storyteller.

According to Long, the model of *witness* incorporates the strengths of all three of the other models. The witness engages the intellect, the emotions, and the imagination. The witness offers a clear message from God, directed to the specific needs and challenges of listeners, by inviting them into stories of God at work in the world, in biblical times as well as today. And key to that engagement is a compelling sermon form. Long integrates this attention to form with attention to other concerns of preachers. Indeed, the abiding popularity of *The Witness of Preaching* is due in part to Long's crystal clear, three-fold, alliterative list of elements to consider in the course of preparing a sermon. He writes that preachers should craft a *focus* (Long's name for a single sentence that states the claim the text makes on the preacher and the people that is brief, theologically balanced, and recognizably related to the biblical text from which it arises), a *function* (Long's word for the specific purpose a preacher has for a specific sermon), and a *form* (Long's word for the patterned communication plan for the sermon). The importance of form is not that it stands alone but that it is so deeply connected to focus and function.

Form Follows Function:
The Purpose of the Sermon Shapes the Form of the Sermon

I continue to use *The Witness of Preaching* as the primary textbook in my Introduction to Preaching classes because it offers the clearest depiction I've encountered anywhere of how form arises from focus. Long charts the move from discerning the theme (focus or claim) of the sermon to shaping the communication plan (form) by which the preacher plans to convey that theme. He acknowledges that the Holy Spirit is at work and at play through-out the whole process of sermon preparation and delivery but refuses to let the preacher attribute sermon form solely to divine alchemy. Instead he leads the preacher through a disciplined process that consists of breaking down the focus into the tasks the preacher needs to accomplish to bring it to fulfillment.

He sets the homiletical buffet table with what he calls a "variety of faithful forms." These include Lowry's narrative loop, Mitchell's account of celebration, Paul Scott Wilson's "four pages," and Craddock's inductive, detective-novel form. Most of these forms join analysis of what is problematic about our current habits and thinking to concrete examples, an offering of God's character or actions that reshapes this problematic situation, and an attempt to say why all this matters.

With all the options available to us in the second decade of the twenty-first century, many preachers still remain fuzzy about form. After a sharp hook in our sermon's opening, we too often meander into the vast morass of the sermon's middle section as, one by one, listeners check out and travel more compelling mental paths of their own making. Or, after an engaging opening and a good effort at holding attention throughout the midsection of the sermon, we then circle the airport in endless over-explanation, unable to land the plane. As Roman Catholic homiletician Ken Unterer says, "Ending a sermon well is like trying to get out of a canoe gracefully!"[7]

In his *The Witness of Preaching*, Long advises preachers to match their endings to the theme (focus) and purpose (function) of the sermon, both in logic and emotional tone. This is his version of the commonsense advice of fiction writers for endings—that they should grow out of the beginning and the middle. The ending, rather than being at cross purposes with the function of the sermon, ought to be the compelling capstone to the form of the entire sermon, carefully crafted to achieve the particular function the preacher has chosen for the sermon. If the function is to challenge and make people think, we end with a question to spur further reflection rather than offering a facile answer to a thorny issue. If it is to call to action in response to a moral crisis in the community, we end with an exhortation to action in the context of hope. If its purpose is to reassure listeners of the faithful qualities of God, we end with a cogent, brief summary statement rather than launching into the history of theological objections to the notion that God is both good and powerful. If the function is to inspire people to a particular action, we end with a story of an individual or group engaging in that behavior, rather than a list of all the reasons one ought to engage in that action. If the function of the sermon is to stir emotions on the way to a change in attitude or actions, we end with eloquent, poetic language, perhaps a familiar hymn or Bible verse, not a summary of points. As preachers following the dictum that "form follows function," we are careful to shape the form of our sermons' endings in such a way as to accomplish the function we intend the sermon to serve.

Form Follows Function:
The Literary Genre Shapes the Form of the Sermon

In 1983 Long wrote an essay and sermon for the anthology *Preaching Biblically: Creating Sermons in the Shape of Scripture*, edited by Don M. Wardlaw. Long's essay was titled "Shaping the Sermon by Plotting the Text's Claim on Us." It was followed by "Exegetical Observations" on Mark 11:11–25 and a sermon on that passage titled "Figs Out of Season." Several years later he published the fruits of his extended reflection on biblical genres' role in shaping sermon form in *Preaching and the Literary Forms of the Bible*. The central argument of both the essay and the book is that the sermon should reflect not just some abstracted "content" of the biblical text but also the genre or literary form of the text.

We've seen how homileticians in the '70s and '80s shifted the locus of meaning-making in the sermon from the speaker to the listener. Long, influenced by the reader response literary criticism of Stanley Fish, Wolfgang Iser, and others, makes a parallel shift from the author to the reader of texts. He calls for preachers to attend to the literary features of various genres of texts and the rhetorical dynamics by which they seek not only to say something but also to do something, to have some impact on the reader. He employs biblical scholar John Barton's definition of genre as "a conventional pattern, recognizable by certain formal criteria (style, shape, tone, syntactic structure, formulaic patterns, etc.) used in a particular society in particular social contexts governed by certain form conventions."[8] Long devotes chapters to psalms, proverbs, narratives, parables, and epistles.

He offers five questions to guide the hermeneutical and homiletical process.

1. What is the genre of the text?
2. What is the rhetorical function of this genre?
3. What literary devices does this genre use to achieve its rhetorical effect?
4. How does this text, in its own literary setting, embody the dynamics described in 1–3?
5. How may the sermon in a new setting say and do what the text says and does in its setting?

He reasons that a sermon on a text of some particular genre should seek to say and do in today's context that which the text sought to say and do in its own context. This kind of preaching requires close attention to—and perhaps even adoption of—the genre of the text.

Long's questions had a strong impact on my own research in the field of homiletics. In the second year of my doctoral coursework, in the fall of 1990, I enrolled in a course on interpreting genres of Old Testament literature for contemporary congregations. It was team-taught by Patrick Miller and Thomas Long. Long's newly published book, *Preaching and the Literary Forms of the Bible*, was one of the texts for the class. I was late for class the week the clipboard went around on which each student signed up to write a thirty-page paper on what was involved in preaching some particular genre. By the time the clipboard came around to me, someone had already purloined the psalms. Another student had nabbed the patriarchal narratives. Yet another had appropriated the apocalyptic texts. Someone had even lapped up the legal codes. The lone genre with no name beside it was proverbs. A classmate quipped, "Good luck getting a sermon out of a one-liner!"

Of course, as a teacher myself, I don't recommend that students arrive late for class. But in this instance, my tardiness had a positive outcome. A Presbyterian friend even suggested that it was providential! I can't speak definitively to that, but I will say that exploring proverbs turned out to be a win-win situation for me for two reasons: first, they have tremendous homiletical potential; and second, they had the shortest bibliography of all the Old Testament genres. I went home that night and read Long's chapter on proverbs in *Preaching and the Literary Forms of the Bible*. I was intrigued by his insight that proverbs are a "risky rhetorical genre" because "they depend to a high degree on the discernment of the reader/hearer to find an apt fit between the proverb and new situations." Guided by his five hermeneutical, homiletical questions, I wrote a paper that explored homiletical models for preaching on proverbs, discovering that, in fact, it was quite possible to get a sermon out of a one-liner!

Long encouraged me to pursue the topic, and with his wise and skillful direction, it eventually became a dissertation that resulted in a book titled *Preaching Proverbs: Wisdom for the Pulpit*.[9] *Preaching and the Literary Forms of the Bible* continued to inspire homileticians through the next two decades as they explored the dynamics of shaping sermons to the forms of the biblical text on which they were based.

"The Times They Are A-Changin'": The Cultural Context Shapes the Form of the Sermon

Over the past couple of decades, homileticians have come to see the ways that the identity of the preacher, the purpose of the sermon, and the literary genre of the texts all matter for the form of the sermon. In recent years homileticians have given more and more attention to the cultural context of the sermon. Context, too, matters for form.

The present context presents at least three challenges to preachers that affect the way we shape our sermons. The first challenge we face is that many people in our pews do not have the "Theology 101" and "Bible 101" that preachers assumed in their listeners at the beginning of the "New Homiletic." The impact of this challenge on sermon form is that sermons today need a greater dose of basic teaching than in a past generation. Inductive preaching calls on a background knowledge in listeners that can no longer be presumed.

The second challenge is the fact that people both within the church walls and beyond them may have lost the skill of making a coherent narrative out of the disparate events of their lives from day to day. Inductive narrative preaching counted on this basic story-making skill being present in their listeners so that they could place biblical stories in the context of their own ongoing life narratives. Now, Long suggests, this narrative competence is more a goal than an ability. The impact of this challenge on sermon form is that sermons need to help people make more direct connections between their lives and the biblical story.

The third challenge is the fact that many people are not buying a Christian metanarrative of salvation that moves from creation to fall to redemption to new creation. They say, "The plotline seems too tidy," or "Church people are too judgmental." Or they claim, "I'm spiritual but not religious," a position Long aptly identifies in *Preaching from Memory to Hope* as a form of Gnosticism marked by its disdain for embodied communal expressions of religion and its excision of eschatology from the Christian narrative.

The "New Homiletic" was undergirded by the conviction that people are inherently story-makers, that we are all engaged in the process of making a coherent narrative out of the disjointed events of our daily lives. A favorite reference of new homileticians was an article by Stephen Crites, then Professor of Religion at Wesleyan University, titled "The Narrative Quality of Experience."[10] In this article Crites argues that the fundamental way humans process experience through time is through narrative. This claim seemed persuasive in the heyday of the New Homiletic. But as we move deeper into the twenty-first century, more and more critics challenge the idea that narrative is the primary means through which we process our lives. In an essay titled "Out of the Loop: The Changing Practice of Preaching," Long explores some of these objections, focusing especially on the theories of British analytic philosopher and literary critic Galen Strawson. Strawson argues that people can process their lives either diachronically or episodically. People who rely on diachronic modes seek to craft coherent narratives of the events of their lives. People who shape their experience through episodic modes live from moment to moment, immersed in the present without trying to connect it with the past or the future. Long challenges this dichotomy, asserting that we are all diachronics but that our attention-deficit, high-tech, visual culture has eroded our ability to exercise our skills at crafting a coherent narrative of our lives. He suggests that many people are living in "random bursts," with "attention fleeting from American Idol to the troop movements in the Middle East to the desire to purchase a more powerful cell phone," all in "a kind of cultural attention deficit disorder."[11]

With these cultural developments in mind, Long notes the resurgence of the didactic, propositional form of preaching in the last couple of decades. This resurgence seems to me to be a response to both the first and second challenges I've mentioned: biblical ignorance and loss of narrative competency in processing life. Now referred to as the "teaching sermon," it is three points and a poem renamed by Long as "six points and a video clip." While Long sees a need for added attention to the educational component of our sermons, he fears that the "teaching sermon" may be an overcorrection. It may "reinforce the worst tendencies of an episodic culture, encouraging people to grasp disconnected principles and rules and insight, provided by an authority figure from the outside, in order to survive in the chaotic whirlwind of life."[12]

While I still unfold my sermons in a more or less inductive manner, more plot-driven than point-driven, I am more intentional these days about articulating and reiterating the stages of the plot as the sermon unfolds. And, without giving the congregation a "honey-do" list every Sunday, I tend to be more directive in my endings than I have been in the past.

Like Long, I would hate to see us overcorrect and abandon the key lessons of the New Homiletic. Deductive, static points are not the only vehicle for biblical and theological insights. Sermons need plots, not just points. Images, metaphors, and stories can inform the intellect as well as touch emotions. Sermons are invitations into a transformative relationship with God, not just vehicles of explanation and information. Highly effective sermons touch emotions and shape imaginations even as they convey robust teaching content. And they often start with a story, image, or metaphor that has been drawn from Scripture and/or life. Out of that story they develop a conceptual thread (focus) that unifies the sermon from start to finish. This kind of preaching—both inductive and deductive, appealing to both diachronic and episodic ways of being in the world—seems like the form of preaching that fits the times.

Form Follows Function:
Making a Scene in the Pulpit

In response to these three challenges—lack of exposure to biblical and theo-logical concepts, suspicion of the Christian metanarrative, and episodic pro-cessing of life's experiences—I would propose a form that I call "scenic" preaching. While people may be resistant to our metanarrative because it seems too good to be true, because they perceive Christians to be judgmental hypocrites, or because they are spiritual but not religious, people still love scenes. While people may be episodic, living in the present, having lost the panoramic vision of their lives, they love devices the size of their palms and being drawn into the scenes that play out there. Our love of scenes is why movies use trailers. It's why YouTube has three billion video views a day, more than twenty-five times the audience of the Super Bowl. It's why every minute forty-eight hours of new video is uploaded. People get drawn into the whole emotional spectrum of scenes, from brutal to humorous to touching: a beheading, a pigeon stealing a bag of Doritos from a convenience store, or a dog helping a puppy down the stairs. People love scenes. They love to post and view scenes from everyday life.

The dynamic of preaching in scenes is an activation of the rhetorical func-tion of narrative that Long describes in *Preaching and the Literary Forms of the Bible*. Stories help us give "logical and meaningful shape to the otherwise incoherent occurrence of events." Stories invite us to become one of the char-acters and/or challenge us to make a decision about the nature of life and how we will live it.[13]

A scene is a freeze-frame in the flow of a story that is composed of a sequence of scenes. A scene is the action that takes place in one physical loca-tion in continuous time. Scenic preaching breaks the story into bite-sized por-tions, focusing on the setting, characters, conflict, plot, and theme of that one scene. It can be a contemporary scene, say, of an elderly bear I once saw at a zoo still pacing the confines of its former cage. It can be a biblical scene, say, of the older brother hovering outside the party. In either case, the preacher invites the listener into the scene and teaches, inspires, and challenges by reference to the elements of that scene. If it is a biblical scene, the preacher makes connec-tions with contemporary life. If it is a contemporary scene, the preacher makes connections with analogous biblical scenes and themes. Once listeners are in the scene, the preacher can point them to the larger story and do some teaching, but from the specific vantage point of this scene and in terms of the elements of narrative (like setting, character, and plot).

Since every scene is preceded by one scene and followed by another, the scenic sermon both speaks to the scenes from which listeners come to worship and to those they go to from worship, equipping them to play their part in their own next scene with more courage and grace as a result of having been drawn into the sermonic scene.

Long's appreciation for form in general and his focus on genre-shaped preaching in particular have shaped my understanding of scenic preaching. He offers a clear and compelling description of the nuanced differences among several genres (psalms, proverbs, narrative, epistles, and parables). This sparks in my mind the insight that they all involve scenes, just scenes with different intended impacts. Proverbs are descriptions of scenes, distilled from observations of repeated patterns of cause and effect observed by the sages. "A soft answer turns away wrath, but a harsh word stirs up anger" (Prov. 15:1). "Like somebody who takes a passing dog by the ears is one who meddles in the quarrel of another" (Prov. 26:17). Their rhetorical intention is ethical teaching.

Long points out that the dynamic of Jesus' parables is to "draw the reader into the world of the parable through identification with one of the characters or through a powerful set of images."[14] Their intended rhetorical impact is to evoke the world of the mysterious Kingdom of God with its ability to reverse habitual assumptions.

The scenic connection is clearest with proverbs, parables, and narrative. But it is also discernible in epistles and psalms. Epistles use the familiarity of the direct address letter format to draw listeners (readers) into a relationship of intimacy to engage in a dialogue in which faith may be strengthened and false teachings questioned. Psalms use the compressed power of poetic language to invite lament, thanksgiving, confession, and praise. While not directly narrative in form, epistles and psalms have a story underlying their writing and offer powerful images from which we can spin scenes of our own. In the psalms a deer longs for flowing streams (Ps. 42) and the psalmist lifts his or her eyes to the hills as a source of danger or protection (Ps. 121) and imagines being sheltered under the divine wings (Ps. 17:8). In various epistles Paul offers us metaphors of a marathon race (Phil. 3:12), a thorn in the flesh (2 Cor. 12:7), and creation groaning in labor pains (Rom. 8:22). Time and space in this essay do not allow the elaboration of all the images and scenes from all the genres with which the two Testaments of the Christian Bible abound.

But we have fifty-two weeks in every year and plenty of opportunities to preach well-formed sermons, sermons shaped to address our listeners in vivid, specific ways: sermons that offer ethical guidance to seekers of wisdom (proverbs); sermons that challenge our narrow, self-centered assumptions (parables); sermons that invite appropriate personal and communal responses to our gracious, reliable God (psalms); and sermons that inspire confidence in the ultimate victory of divine justice as it plays out from day to day (apocalyptic).

At the end of his essay "Out of the Loop," Long makes this comment about our vocation as preachers in relation to sermon forms for the future:

> We are called to proclaim a narrative that people could not conjure up out of their own resources, the gospel narrative, and then to help people let that narrative become the story that shapes, guides, and clarifies their lives and gives them their primary identity. No single homiletical formula will do; no one way of structuring sermons, however compelling, will accomplish the task; no solitary rhetorical strategy will open all the doors of the faithful imaginations of our hearers. . . . We must use every gift of language, every responsible strategy of communication, to help people see, in practical and concrete ways, the shape of life that results when one builds a nest in the wide and embracing branches of the gospel story.[15]

Long's teaching, writing, and preaching have done just this work. They have helped students, pastors, and laypeople shape their lives by the gospel narrative, letting it become the story that "shapes, guides and clarifies their lives and gives them their primary identity."

A student of mine, schooled in my Introduction to Preaching class in the methods of *The Witness of Preaching,* told of a sermon she preached recently. At the door a woman, her eyes glistening with tears, took her hand and said, "Thank you! I was able to follow your sermon from start to finish and you gave me something to take home!" To which my student replied, "Don't thank me; thank Tom Long!"

Chapter 3

Crafting a Sermon Series

Contemporary Approaches to Structuring Preaching over Time

SCOTT BLACK JOHNSTON

How should contemporary clergy organize their preaching over the long haul? Is the lectionary still the best bet? Or is it growing tired? Is it possible to design a sermon series that has both theological integrity and cultural relevance?

*O*ne of the great joys and burdens of preaching is Monday morning. Completing another turn in the pulpit brings a sense of fulfillment and respite. Worshipping together as a community of faith immerses us again in God's profound grace. And yet, the stone that the preacher rolled up the hill is once again at the bottom. On Monday mornings, preachers face the inevitable return of Sunday, and with it the question: What next? What biblical text will I study this week? What congregational concerns will I attempt to address? What am I going to preach about now?

These questions have been around for thousands of years. In response, communities of faith have developed calendars of readings. They have subdivided the witness of Scripture so as to structure time in a liturgical manner. These calendars provide a clear answer to the question, "What's next?" We can see this practice on display in the Gospel of Luke. When Jesus walks into the synagogue in Nazareth he is handed the scroll of Isaiah (Luke 4:17). He does not request Isaiah but participates in the custom of teaching from the text appointed for the day. You might even say that, on this occasion, Jesus preached from a lectionary—a calendar of readings.

In North America, there are many Christian traditions that do not prescribe or follow a lectionary. For those that do, the most popular calendar structuring weekly preaching over the last forty years has been the Revised Common Lectionary (RCL). This essay explores an alternative to the RCL: the locally designed sermon series. While the RCL will remain a valued homiletical option for many preachers, the use of a clergy-devised local sermon series can provide a healthy alternative to (or occasional supplement for) the RCL in organizing preaching over the long haul.

The Revised Common Lectionary

The popularity of the RCL is well deserved. In existence in various forms since 1969, the RCL offers a set of readings (Old Testament, Psalm, Epistle, and Gospel) that follow the liturgical year. These texts expose preachers and congregations to the breadth of Scripture while building a sturdy liturgical scaffold for preaching over time.

The primary logic of the RCL is Christological.[1] It provides an annual, cyclical framework for exploring the life and teachings of Jesus with a congregation. As such, the RCL often uses a passage from one of the four Gospels as the focal text and then chooses other biblical texts as evocative conversation partners for this central passage.[2] In the RCL, this Christological pattern is most clearly evident in the Advent-Christmas-Epiphany cycle and the Lent-Holy Week-Easter cycle.

While primary, Christology is not the only theological impulse guiding the RCL. The RCL also provides texts for doctrinal feast days (e.g., Trinity Sunday) and other liturgical observances (e.g., Ash Wednesday). Throughout most of the year (Ordinary Time), the RCL offers a schedule of continuous reading (*lectio continua*) that leads congregations and preachers on an uninterrupted trip through various Epistles and Old Testament books without trying to forge a connection between these passages and the Gospel text for the day.

Preachers working with the RCL realize numerous benefits:

- It streamlines the process of text selection.
- It leads preachers and congregations to encounter portions of Scripture they might otherwise miss or avoid.
- It follows the contours of the liturgical year—the Christian calendar.
- Its recognized framework facilitates communal study of biblical texts with colleagues.
- It can provide a sense of Christian unity across a wider community. When preachers in various churches within a locality address the same set of texts, they plant the seeds for (and equip parishioners to have) engaging conversations about the faith in the broader public square.
- Finally, the RCL is extremely well resourced by periodicals, commentaries, hymnals, and an ever-expanding menu of helpful websites and blogs.

Despite these many benefits, the format of the RCL leaves it open to legitimate and important criticisms. In selecting biblical texts based on a narrow set of theological criteria, in cutting passages down to a "readable" size, and in deciding what texts are best set in conversation with other "parallel" texts and liturgical days, the lectionary inevitably ignores a hefty chunk of Scripture. The choices made by the RCL, in the words of Thomas G. Long, result in "the practical constriction of the full canon of Scripture in the preaching of the church."[3]

To combat this "constriction," Long urges preachers to read both before and after the passages assigned by the RCL in order to get a sense of the assigned text in the larger flow of Scripture in which it is found.[4] Seeking to address related concerns, Timothy Matthew Slemmons has authored *Year D: A Quadrennial Supplement to the Revised Common Lectionary*. This helpful addition to the RCL exposes preachers and congregations to portions of Scripture (like the psalms of lament and apocalyptic material) that are sorely underrepresented in the RCL.[5]

Although good faith attempts have been made to fix the RCL's selective engagement with Scripture by expanding the current set of passages and providing alternative reading tracks, three persistent criticisms continue to be voiced by contemporary clergy.

First, preachers complain that when they return for the third or fourth time to the same set of lectionary texts, the creative process can feel forced. I recently heard a preacher confess that she began to study the familiar RCL passages for the upcoming Advent season with a sense of weariness. In response to such comments, RCL proponents often assert that biblical texts have a surplus of meaning, and as such, no one sermon (or series of sermons) can exhaust a particular passage.

This is of course true. Yet it provides little relief to preachers who report a growing sense of tedium after following the RCL for repeated cycles. The above-mentioned preacher felt that her options were either: (a) plowing the same ground again or (b) trying to develop obscure interpretations for her listeners. Exasperated, she asked a group of colleagues: "Does anybody have a viable alternative for Advent that will keep both me and the congregation engaged?" We will return to her important question.

A second criticism of the RCL is that the Sunday-to-Sunday flow of texts can, during certain key seasons, feel bewildering to those who have less grounding in the overall biblical narrative. For example, in Advent, the RCL hopscotches from predictions of Christ's return in Revelation, back to Old Testament messianic texts, then forward to John the Baptist, before finally getting to Mary and Joseph. At times, the RCL requires that preachers spend significant time connecting the dots—explaining why this particular text has been chosen for this particular day and how it relates to the texts being used in previous and subsequent Sundays. This energy can be time well spent. While it may seem confusing to listeners, there are blessings to be had in exploring the contours of Advent hope as laid out in the RCL. At other times, however, preachers can feel that this is second-order homiletical work. In other words, there are times when the lectionary seems to depend on listeners who have a fairly intimate knowledge of Scripture. Increasingly, this is not the case. As such, preachers argue that before they can unpack the theological logic of an Advent journey through the RCL, they need to assist the congregation to find a solid footing in the first two chapters of the Gospel of Luke.

A third persistent criticism of the RCL is that the liturgical assumptions forming the backbone of the lectionary pay little heed to local realities. Yes, an interesting conversation can almost always be cultivated between any random biblical text and a preacher's local context. More often than not, however, the hermeneutical gymnastics necessary to forge such a connection prove distracting to listeners. There are times that call for a biblical text with a clear and more direct connection to issues being faced by a local community than is provided by the RCL.

Preachers know this in their bones. Every day, clergy think about how their sermons can faithfully support and advance things like a community-wide conversation on race and faith, a building campaign to renovate a sanctuary, or a new youth ministry initiative. These concerns lead us back to our core question: How can a preacher craft a short-term, locally focused preaching plan that will speak with relevance and truth? How does one go about designing a faithful sermon series?

Sermon Series Design

Designing a cohesive and engaging sermon series takes time. Many contemporary preachers report that they regularly dedicate blocks of time during the summer and after major holidays to draft upcoming sermon series. This investment in homiletical research and design is crucial to pulling together a blueprint that will: (1) embody a clear goal for the series, (2) provide a logical progression of ideas (or, at least, help avoid redundancy), and (3) provide a jumping off place for the preacher over the coming weeks in preparing each of the sermons.

As a preacher begins the design process, the following questions may prove helpful:

- What type of series am I designing? What approach is best suited for the subject matter I have in mind and the congregational context in which I am embedded?
- When should I schedule it? How long will the series be?
- How do I select the biblical texts that will undergird the series? How do I pair biblical texts with topics?
- What other congregation events or activities might help support or might grow out of the sermon series?
- How do I publicize the series?

To start answering these questions, let's survey the types of localized sermon series being offered by contemporary preachers.[6]

The Hot Topic

There are times in ministry when pressing issues and questions in the wider culture warrant more concentrated homiletical attention than a single sermon. In these moments, taking our cues from educators who are adept at curriculum design, preachers may decide to design a sermon series that will unpack the various theological and cultural facets of a complicated and contentious issue for listeners. Engaging in pedagogy with a purpose, these preachers seek to equip people in faith communities for graceful, theologically informed dialogue with one other and with their neighbors in the public square.

Given our natural interest in hot topics (e.g., income inequality, race and criminal justice, or same-sex marriage), it is no surprise when they quickly become fodder for countless news programs, editorials, and water-cooler conversations. These omnipresent conversations mean that these issues are often at the forefront of people's minds when they arrive for weekly worship. What is a preacher to do with this potentially volatile combination of conviction and curiosity? Should I preach on this subject? And if so, how?

In recent years, some preachers have chosen to dial down their prophetic voice, citing recent surveys by The Pew Foundation in which congregants state that they disapprove of preachers who take overly "political" positions in the pulpit.[7] These surveys warrant close study. What exactly do parishioners mean by "political" sermons? According to Pew, listeners are most distressed when preachers identify a particular political party or political movement as being "righteous" while assessing another party or candidate as "unrighteous."

Savvy participants in the wider culture, sermon listeners see religious endorsement for a politician, a platform, or a party as unwise. Over the years, congregants have watched parties and politicians exploit voters' passions in unscrupulous ways. They do not want their clergy to be lured into a tainted relationship with the powers and principalities. This does not mean, however, that listeners want their preachers to fall silent on controversial issues. On the contrary, Pew reports that the faithful are deeply interested in hearing preachers grapple with the issues of the day. They yearn to be equipped to think about these topics through the lens of their faith.

With that in mind, preachers bold enough to address a controversial issue in a sermon series are not simply offering theological and cultural analysis; they are also modeling the ethics of Christian communication for their congregation. They demonstrate courage in breaking the silence. At their best, they show forth grace and love even as they pursue justice. They lift up the values of diversity by honoring differing points of view and refusing to offer caricatures. Even as these preachers present what is theologically at stake with clarity and passion, they provide powerful models for how Christians can engage each other (and their neighbors) in difficult issues.

The Expository Series

All sermon series do not necessarily use a contemporary topic as a point of departure. Today, some of the most common (and most popular) series take their cues from the expository *lectio continua* tradition practiced by such ancient luminaries as St. Augustine.

The expository series focuses on a particular biblical book (e.g., Exodus) or a section of a book (e.g., patriarchs and matriarchs in Gen. 12–50). An expository series may also focus on a genre (e.g., the parables of Jesus) or multiple genres grouped under a larger literary category (e.g., psalms).

When sketching the blueprint for an expository sermon series, the overall design is strengthened when a preacher establishes a clear goal for the series. Is the purpose pedagogical? Does the preacher plan to do a close reading of a biblical text to better acquaint listeners with a discrete portion of Scripture? (Augustine famously preached thirteen sermons on John 16!) Or is the goal to assist listeners in adopting a particular genre (like the psalms) for use in their devotional lives? Or is there some other purpose?

In an expository series, preachers often seek to expose congregants to the depth and variety manifest by such texts. Again, taking the book of Psalms as an example, the preacher might consider using psalms that are representative of various sub-genres (e.g., an individual lament, a communal lament, a psalm of ascent, a psalm of deliverance, a psalm of thanksgiving, and so on).

A sermon series on the parables would, in a similar fashion, do well to present a variety of different types of parables, thus exposing listeners to the rich landscape of this literary form.

The Topical/Expository Hybrid

Another common series format results when a preacher places a local theological question or issue in conversation with a particularly well-suited biblical conversation partner. Imagine a congregation grappling with a set of questions related to ecclesial identity: What is the church? What is our relationship to the surrounding culture? What ethics should govern our interactions with each other and the world around us? Using an expository/topical hybrid model, the preacher might decide to preach a sermon series that wrestles with these critical questions while journeying through the Bible's account of the early church—the Acts of the Apostles.

Or imagine a church that is struggling with a loss of influence and prestige in relation to the culture while at the same time expressing concerns about fragmentation in the social fabric and the plight of the poor. This pastor may well decide that a journey through the book of Jeremiah might afford her an opportunity to address some of the community's questions while at the same time equipping congregants with a crucial resource from our tradition.

The Congregational Response Series

Increasingly, preachers use a sermon series to respond to topics, texts, or concerns that are directly submitted by congregation members. Contemporary clergy have constructed sermon series based on "Your Favorite Biblical Passages," "Ten Questions Our Youth Have for the Church," and "Our Eight Favorite Hymns." Obviously, series like this work best when the congregation is broadly solicited for input and provided with accessible avenues for submitting responses.

The congregational response sermon series provides clergy with a concrete way of accomplishing something that Thomas G. Long encourages preachers to pursue with intentionality. We must not forget, he writes, "that we rise to the pulpit from the pew"—bringing with us listeners' questions and concerns so that they might be placed in conversation with the Christian tradition.[8] Thomas Are Jr., pastor of Village Presbyterian Church in Kansas City, observes that this approach to preaching embodies the "incarnational impulse" that produced the New Testament. The biblical writers all saw that word as becoming flesh in unique ways in their context of ministry. Matthew edits Mark because he has different people in his pews and needs to respond to their particular questions and concerns. Paul's letters are theological responses to very concrete issues in very different communities. A series that begins with the congregation as a starting point is an extension of our tradition's deep belief that we must always be responding theologically to the concerns on the street and in the pews.

The Doctrinal Series

Seeing both classic and contemporary formulations of Christian doctrine as guiding expressions of people's faith and ethical lives, today's preachers are also developing sermon series framed around doctrinal issues. Some have worked their way, clause by clause, through classic documents like the Apostles' Creed and the Nicene Creed. Others have taken a more contemporary document like the Belhar Confession (a statement written by churches resisting the apartheid regime in South Africa) as an opportunity to preach about the circumstances giving rise to the faith statement as well as an exposition of the theological themes contained in the document. Still others have taken a doctrine like the Trinity and framed a series that walks with listeners on a journey from the earliest formulations of this core doctrine all the way to contemporary understandings of God's inherently relational nature. Finally, some contemporary preachers have once again embraced classic creeds like the Heidelberg Catechism, recognizing that confessions like this were structured with preaching over the long term in mind. The Heidelberg Catechism provides a set of doctrinal sermon topics meant to last a preacher one calendar year.

The Liturgical Series

While the RCL has a wonderful track record connecting listeners with the rhythms of the liturgical year, there are sermon series that emphasize elements of communal worship that do not have a natural home in the RCL.

Earlier, we took note of a question posed by a preacher who felt weary as she contemplated one more pass through a rather familiar set of Advent texts: "Is there another way to do this creatively and faithfully?" There is good news for this preacher to be found in locally developed sermon series;

for, it turns out, there are actually numerous faithful ways to walk through Advent.

Jon Walton, pastor of First Presbyterian Church in the City of New York, developed an innovative Advent sermon series after hearing Tom Long describe the Gospel writers as people living at the four corners of the same intersection but in very different types of houses. Running with this, Walton designed a series that looks sequentially at the Incarnation from the perspectives of each of the four Gospels. Instead of sticking with one Gospel throughout Advent (as the RCL tends to do), Walton imagined what Christmas might look like, first at Mark's house, then at Matthew's house, then at Luke's house, and finally at John's house. In each case, Walton pictures a home festooned and populated in a way that reflects the incarnational theology espoused by that particular Gospel.

Mark's house is austere and focuses on the adult Jesus and his crucifixion. Luke's house is open to all sorts of people—boisterous low-income shepherds and singing women. Matthew hosts a massive family reunion; everyone is gathered around a table, poring over a genealogy. And so on. Throughout the series, Walton's creative twist proves engaging, but it is also theologically eye-opening. Listeners are given a chance to contemplate how each Gospel anticipates the arrival of Jesus in a unique way. The implicit question undergirding the series is: What house feels like home to you? What is your incarnational theology? Walton's approach to Advent has been adopted and customized by numerous other clergy around the country.

Other preachers seeking a liturgically focused approach to structuring their preaching over time have developed sermon series focused on the elements of worship. In other words, they have preached a sermon on "The Call to Worship," a sermon on "Hymn Singing," a sermon on "The Prayer of Confession," a sermon on "The Offering" (on Stewardship Sunday!), and so on. Another popular approach involves a series of sermons that exegete the furniture and architecture of worship: a sermon on the baptismal font, the communion table, the pulpit, the nave, and other elements in the space of worship.

The Historical Series

The history of God's people is another field providing fertile ground for preachers contemplating sermon series. At Trinity United Church of Christ in Chicago, Dr. Otis Moss III has developed a powerful annual series that coincides with Black History Month. Over four weeks, Moss traces the route of the Maafa. *Maafa* is a Swahili word meaning "disaster" or "holocaust." The term has come to refer to the history of the slave trade and the long legacy of atrocities against the African diaspora that have happened in its wake.

On the first Sunday of Black History Month, Moss begins his sermon series in West Africa—in a country from which people were abducted into slavery. Using the language and music of the chosen country to set the liturgical context, Moss preaches a sermon that tells the story of a specific West African culture that was afflicted by violent marauders who kidnapped its children. On the second Sunday of the month, Moss follows the enslaved persons as they cross the ocean in chains and arrive in the West Indies. On the third Sunday, the sermon and the liturgy follow the enslaved people to a location in the American South. On the fourth Sunday, the sermon follows African Americans on the Great Migration (1910–1970), moving from the rural South to the urban Northeast, Midwest, and West. On each Sunday, the music used in worship mirrors the context of the journey, beginning with traditional African, moving to Caribbean, then turning to the roots of American Gospel, and finally considering the Blues. In each sermon in the series, says Moss, "I seek to connect listeners to an ancestral heritage in which God has stood by us through one of the most horrific events in human history."

Other Options

Some preachers have designed sermon series that are ecclesial in nature: a series on the "Marks of the Church," a series on Reformation figures, a series on the founding of a church with subsequent sermons on milestone events and challenging moments in that church's history. Preachers have constructed sermon series that address questions facing religion and science. Others have preached multiple sermons on stewardship during that season of the church year.

I recently developed a series on idolatry. Citing Paul Tillich's observation that God is the name we give to our "ultimate concern," I asked the congregation to think about the ultimate concerns that shaped their own ethics and the ethics of those with whom they worked, went to school, and lived. The congregation's thoughtful responses were paired with classic biblical texts on idolatry. The result was a series titled "New York Gods."

Other preachers have modeled local sermon series on the oft-revived and popular *Christian Century* articles titled, "How My Mind Has Changed." In this series, editors have asked famous theologians and scholars to reflect on the courses of their careers and lift up places where their thoughts have changed on a matter of some significance. One preacher remarked that his congregation found that this particular series served to both humanize the church's clergy and liberate their own faith.

Truly, the possibilities for creative and faithful sermon series are limited only by a preacher's imagination.

How Many Weeks and When?

I suggest setting the maximum length for a sermon series at twelve weeks. This span of time is long enough to give the preacher and the congregation time to adequately explore a topic or set of biblical texts before (hopefully) either party becomes fatigued with the subject. The framers of the RCL (and even further back, the Christian liturgical year) had their own sense of the church's communal attention span when they set seven-week periods for Advent/Christmas, Lent, and Eastertide.

There is wisdom in keeping homegrown series at least as focused as the RCL. Indeed, sermon series do not need to be multiple-month endeavors. Some series are best suited to laser-beam focus. I once preached a two-week series on the religious freedom clause in the First Amendment of the U.S. Constitution. At the time it was a hot topic in the news, and people appreciated a quick faith-based perspective on the issue.

All in all, when determining the length of a sermon series, it is the preacher's responsibility to consider the complexity of the subject matter, to gauge the congregation's level of interest in the topic, and to think strategically about the church's wider calendar.

When is the best time in the church year to preach a sermon series? Some preachers choose to work out of the RCL during Lent/Holy Week/Easter and preach sermon series during the Ordinary Time of summer and fall, during Epiphany, and during Eastertide. Others develop sermon series exclusively for the summer months. Still others organize their entire annual worship schedule around a progression of sermon series of various lengths. Deciding on the timing and frequency of sermon series in a local context, preachers should keep in mind that each series requires advanced planning and study.

How Do I Connect Texts and Topics?

Connecting the topics of a series to biblical texts for the sermons is one of the most challenging aspects in designing a sermon series. In theory, preachers search for texts that will speak in an inspiring and relevant way to the issue at hand. In practice—facing the entire corpus of Scripture—preachers often default to their own favorite texts when seeking a conversation partner for a contemporary issue. In some cases, a familiar text that pops to mind may be the preacher's best option; yet we shouldn't be too quick to step back from one of the clear strengths of the old RCL. Namely, there are many powerful, enlightening texts that fall outside our personal canons. These passages can bless the preacher and the congregation in untold ways, if we have the mettle to engage them.

So how does a preacher go about finding relevant passages outside our standard catalog of texts? Again, I think we can take our cues from Tom Long.[9] Read broadly! Imagine that you are preparing a sermon on stem cell research. Where might you find a biblical text to inform this conversation? If you do an online search for "biblical passages on stem cell research," you will discover sites that identify a "definitive passage"—a text that someone believes makes clear God's will on the matter. Sometimes these searches are helpful. More often than not, though, the Internet's "definitive" guidance comes freighted with its own set of peculiar hermeneutical contortions.

How else might we read broadly? Otis Moss III advocates that preachers adopt an old-school pastoral discipline that will regularly take us into unfamiliar territory and give the Spirit a chance to enter into the homiletical process: read the Bible devotionally. Read it regularly. Read it sequentially. Read it cover to cover, and then start over again. This practice, Moss contends, has resulted in him regularly finding fresh (and often uncommon) texts that speak in surprisingly relevant ways to God's people and the issues of the day.

Another way to find relevant passages of Scripture is to solicit advice from experts in your own congregation. Ask a doctor what her perspective is on stem cell research and inquire if she has reflected on it from a faith stance. See if there is a particular biblical passage that comes to mind when she thinks about the issue. This is also a good time to e-mail clergy friends and former professors. I find, more often than not, that the most interesting and challenging suggestions for connecting a topic and a text come from thoughtful friends and personal devotional reading and not from Internet searches or biblical concordances.

What do you do when the Bible seems to offer conflicting testimony about a subject? Honestly, I advise that you highlight this fact. Listeners either know or should be reminded that the biblical corpus is a complex tapestry—the product of faithful people from vastly different communities and cultures over the course of thousands of years. When we avoid biblical texts that already hold a place in people's minds in regard to a particular subject (e.g., human sexuality), these texts will be quoted to us by congregants on their way out the church door. Why not allow the sermon to recognize with candor those texts that frequently come to mind in regard to this issue? Then the preacher can begin to deepen people's understanding of these texts, too.

What Other Congregation Events/Activities Might Help Support or Might Grow Out of the Sermon Series?

Sermon series present great opportunities for preachers to think creatively about ways to tie in to events in education, interfaith dialogue, outreach, service, and conversations/interactions with neighboring churches and with the local community.

Again, when it comes to controversial issues, preachers are encouraged to remember that a sermon is primarily a one-way mode of communication. It is a monologue. The more controversial the topic, the more important it is for the church to provide a time of ongoing conversation for all members of the community immediately after worship. In advance of a sermon on a hot topic, it can be very helpful to schedule a meal and to train table hosts who will be prepared to draw listeners into a space of candid, safe, and gracious dialogue about the issue.

How Do I Publicize the Series?

Convey your excitement about the series to listeners, and they will respond! Preachers should begin publicizing an upcoming sermon series at least two weeks before it begins. Using church newsletters, website banners, e-mails, and social media, the preacher should craft a short paragraph explaining why he or she chose this sermon series for this moment in time. Preachers should also, throughout the research process, keep their eyes peeled for an image or series of images that captures and illustrates the series' focus. Finally, clergy may even want to recommend some advance reading—like an accessible article—to whet the congregation's spiritual appetite for the subject matter and to begin the larger conversation that the series will nurture.

In Sum

The locally crafted sermon series can provide an exciting, theologically relevant, culturally and contextually aware alternative to the Revised Common Lectionary. Yes, creating a series is labor intensive, but—done well—these series can: (1) engage preachers in fresh textual study, (2) give congregational questions and concerns new status, and (3) help all participate in conversations of consequence regarding God's activity and claim on our lives.

PART II   Theology

Chapter 4

The Blessing of Melchizedek

Preaching in a World of Many Faiths

BARBARA BROWN TAYLOR

How do we preach in a way that affirms Christian theology while also honoring the insights of other faith traditions?

*P*reachers who are interested in the answer to this question may already suspect how many other substantial questions it provokes. Why would a Christian minister honor the insights of another faith before a Christian congregation? What parts of Christian theology might such a sermon call into question? The average college textbook contains introductions to a dozen major world religions. On what grounds will a preacher decide which of their insights are honorable and which are not? What is implied by presenting them as insights instead of truths?

These are such new questions for most Christians that no set answers exist. While they are all theological in nature, they reflect such rapid changes in the religious landscape that the preacher who engages them may be doing theology instead of looking it up. A Presbyterian missionary serving in Indonesia can develop a style that speaks to her multicultural congregation, but she will have to start all over again when she returns to the southern United States. A nondenominational pastor planting a church for millennials in downtown Seattle will operate from a different set of concerns than the Catholic priest assigned to a suburban parish outside of Boston.

In all these places and more, listeners come for different reasons and hear with different ears. For some, a preacher's failure to honor the insights of other religions becomes proof that the church is stuck in its exclusive past. For others, the effort to include wisdom from other traditions is the sure sign that the church has surrendered its singular truth. It is a rare congregation that does not include both kinds of listeners.

Yet these same listeners also listen to news anchors, popular songwriters, talk show hosts, and Facebook friends. They go to movies and watch homemade videos on their computers. Even the youngest among them know how quickly the world changes, as new technologies and new neighbors bring the world into their living rooms. It is no longer surprising to meet Christians who practice yoga and meditation, read books by Deepak Chopra, or follow the Dalai Lama on Twitter. Some went to school with people of other faiths or married them. Others learned to tell the difference between Muslims and Sikhs by serving in the armed forces with them or found out what it means to sit *shiva* when their Jewish boss's father died.

They are not unaware of the ways in which their lives are intertwined with neighbors of other faiths; they simply do not expect to hear anything about that at church—except, perhaps, how important it is that those neighbors be persuaded to become Christian instead. Even in congregations that are more at ease with religious pluralism, there can be an odd disconnect between what Christians do at church and what they do in the rest of their lives.

The Challenges of Change

Before deciding *how* to honor the insights of other traditions in a Christian sermon, preachers need to know *why*. Are fault lines appearing between people of different faiths in the local community? Is news coming in from other parts of the world that threatens to demonize an entire religion? Are prominent Christians saying contradictory things that beg some mediation? Or is it simply time for Christianity to take its place among the world's other great religions with no plan to dominate? These are only a few of the reasons why a preacher might decide to address the teachings of other faiths in a Christian sermon.

In 2005 Robert Wuthnow published a book called *America and the Challenges of Religious Diversity.* As director of the Center for the Study of Religion at Princeton, he was interested in how well a "Christian nation" was doing with increasing numbers of neighbors devoted to other faiths. In order to discover the answer to that question, his team of researchers spoke with almost three thousand people who had been selected as representative of the adult population of the United States. After the initial survey, researchers went back to two hundred of the respondents who were church members to ask more questions about their beliefs and the activities of their churches. Fifty pastors also agreed to interviews that were designed to assess their awareness of and level of interaction with people of other faiths.

In a central chapter of the book titled "How Congregations Manage Diversity," Wuthnow delivered this troubling verdict:

One of the main conclusions that emerges from conversations with scores of pastors in various parts of the country is that many churches—probably a majority—are dealing with the growing religious diversity of our society by simply avoiding the issue. They seldom talk specifically about how to relate to their Jewish, Muslim, Hindu, or Buddhist neighbors and they certainly do not sponsor activities that would bring them into contact with these neighbors. Yet these are churches that are located within a few blocks of mosques, temples, or synagogues and their pastors are thoughtful and informed leaders who are clearly aware that other religions are an increasingly prominent reality in today's world. How is it possible for pastors to avoid paying greater attention to other religions?[1]

Wuthnow went on to identify several pastoral "strategies of avoidance" for dealing with religious pluralism. These included the wish to avoid unnecessary theological trouble ("I think there'd be resistance from the members"), the limits of institutional ministry ("It's just not in line with what we're trying to do here"), and the problem of overall busyness ("It would just be another thing to do"). While it is not possible to read the full list of these excuses without feeling the discomfort of the pastors offering them up, they still add up to a rather long list.

Most of these congregational leaders would not hesitate to become involved if a nearby synagogue were set on fire or a Muslim school threatened. Yet they are often reluctant to take the initiative in building relationships that might lessen the odds of such things happening. Even in my small community where most of the fire is rhetorical, I do not see many letters to the editor from local pastors. Why borrow trouble when there is already enough to go around?

Plus, it is no small thing to construct (much less communicate) a Christian theology of other religions. While most major Christian denominations have published position papers on their relationships to people of other faiths, making sense of those positions requires readers to grapple with difficult questions such as how and to whom God is revealed, who Jesus was and is, what salvation means, and who is eligible for it. While these are central questions of Christian faith, all taken up in standard college introductions to Christian theology, I do not know many churches that explore them in any systematic way.

Small wonder, then, that some Christians question whether engaging neighbors of other faiths is "in line with what we're doing here." Does taking time to learn about other religions legitimate their teachings? If we initiate relationships with people who do not believe in Jesus without trying to change their minds, what does that say about our commitment to the gospel? Are we saying that one religion is as good as another?

The illogic in some of these questions, common as they are, demonstrates not only the need for critical thinking in such matters but also how important it is for Christians to recognize central Christian reasons to engage neighbors of other faiths with no plan to change their minds. This is the point at which the sermon comes clearly into view, since listeners who confess little interest in theology often remain interested in what the Bible says.

The Problem of the Stranger

"You shall love your neighbor as yourself" and "Do unto others as you would have them do unto you" are the twin teachings that are as helpful in this context as any other, though there is plenty to be wondered about which "neighbor" and what "others" Jesus might have had in view. In Luke's Gospel, he declined to define his terms, perhaps sensing that the lawyer's question was meant to limit instead of expand the population of the command (Luke 10:29). Instead, he invented a story that allowed his listeners to answer the question for themselves. That strategy is as shrewd today as it was then, since it asks listeners to imagine a world in which mercy crosses historical boundaries of religion, culture, and class. It also banks on the power of empathy to make that crossing in the face of a hundred hallowed reasons why one should not.

Needless to say, the imaginary priest and Levite in this story cannot be turned into "the Jews" who failed the test of showing mercy. As Amy-Jill Levine clarifies in her book *Short Stories by Jesus,* Samaritans had laws about corpse contamination too.[2] Plus, the priest and Levite were going down from Jerusalem (away from the Temple), not up, rendering their ritual purity irrelevant. Even if they were going up, Torah required both of them to attend to the wounded man regardless of who he was or what they might be doing later in the day. Their failure, she says, was an ordinary one: they knew what was right and they did not do it.

Levine demonstrates the versatility of the teaching by recalling the best explanation of it that she has heard. When Martin Luther King Jr. preached on the parable, he reckoned that the main difference between the three would-be helpers in the story was the question they asked themselves when they first saw the wounded man lying on the ground. For the priest and the Levite, the question was, "If I stop to help this man, what will happen to me?" For the Samaritan, the question was, "If I do not stop to help this man, what will happen to him?" Taking the teaching to heart, King asked himself, "If I do not stop to help the sanitation workers, what will happen to them?" So he went to Memphis to help them, and there a bandit took his life.[3]

This true story serves as a corrective to the ways in which the story of the Good Samaritan has been tamed, turning him into the Ronald McDonald of helping those in any kind of need. The Good Samaritan's name is now on medical centers, neighborhood clinics, relief agencies, job centers, nursing homes, credit unions, and thousands of recreational vehicles—all but obliterating the suspicion of him and "his kind" that made Jesus' story dangerous in the first place.

The problem with retelling this story in the present is that we will have to identify a group regarded with equal suspicion by the congregation in front of us, and this may have the unintended effect of reinforcing a negative stereotype. To single out one member of a group as surprisingly "good" is to imply that the rest are not. Skillful preachers may still find ample reasons to preach sermons on the Good Muslim, the Good Mormon, or the Good Atheist as a way of "outing" the prejudice against neighbors whom Good Christians are least likely to love.

The second general teaching, widely known as the Golden Rule, comes up in the context of Jesus' Sermon on the Mount (Matt. 7:12) and his Sermon on the Plain (Luke 6:31). The virtue of Matthew's account is the equation of Jesus' teaching about "others" with the teaching of the law and the prophets. This natural link to the first testament is the preacher's invitation to learn as much about its teaching on strangers as he or she can, not only as Christians understand it but also as Jews understand it, with the aid of a Talmud that most Christians know next to nothing about.

Preachers who enjoy doing their own digging may begin by searching "stranger" in their favorite concordances, noticing how many ways the word is used in the first thirty-nine books of the Bible. Even those who are fluent in Hebrew will benefit from comparing English translations and being curious about the differences between them. Why does "stranger" get just twenty-five hits in the New Revised Standard Version and eighteen in the New International Version, compared to a whopping sixty-seven in the Jewish Publication Society version? Word searches of "alien" and "neighbor" produce other surprising differences, all of them worth wondering about.

According to Jonathan Sacks, retired Chief Rabbi of the United Hebrew Congregations of Britain and the Commonwealth, Torah contains one command to love the neighbor (Lev. 19:18) and no fewer than thirty-six to love the stranger (beginning with Lev. 19:34). The frequency of these commands bears witness to what Sacks calls "the issue that has proved to be the most difficult in the history of human interaction, namely the problem of the stranger, the one who is not like us."[4]

In his award-winning book *The Dignity of Difference*, published shortly after the events of September 11, 2001, Sacks argues that it is time for people of good faith to do more than search for shared human values. The tired old teaching of tolerance (which was never much good to begin with) cannot bear the weight of rapid globalization. An academic affirmation of religious pluralism is not much better. What we need, Sacks says, is a reinvention at the heart of the monotheistic imagination, where allegiance to the one God has long been understood as allegiance to one faith, one way, and one truth. But what if that understanding misses the mark? What if the real proposition at the heart of monotheism is that unity creates diversity?

The next step, Sacks says, is "not only a theology of commonality—of the universals of mankind—but also a theology of difference: why it exists, why it matters, why it is constitutive of our humanity, why it represents the will of God."[5]

Strangers in the Bible

The story of the tower of Babel in Genesis 11 is a good place to start, since among other things it is a story about the emergence of strangeness among people once united by a common language and purpose.

You remember the basics: the whole earth had one language and used the same words. People were so empowered by this great gift of unanimity that they figured out how to make bricks. Since they were all on the same page and did not need translators to understand one another, it took them only about five minutes to decide to use those bricks to build a city with a tower that would reach to the heavens. Why did they want to do that? In order to "make a name" for themselves, the Bible says, for "otherwise we shall be scattered abroad upon the face of the whole earth" (11:4).

Since there was no dissent among them, everything went according to plan. They set about building the city and the tower with its top in the heavens, but when God discovered what they were doing, God confused their language and scattered them over the face of the earth, just as they had feared. No longer able to understand a word one another said, they left their city unfinished and walked away from it in different directions, never again to speak to one another without finding a translator first.

In the Christian imagination, this story is traditionally heard as a tale of God's judgment on overachieving human beings, with more than a faint echo of the trespass in Eden in it. But that hearing clearly depends on a negative evaluation of diversity. Put that premise in park for a minute, and it may be possible to hear the story as a tale of God's judgment on human sameness.

When everyone is the same—when everyone speaks the same language and sees things the same way—when there is no one to argue with, no one to say, "Are you sure that's a good idea?" or "I don't understand; could you say that a different way?" then one-language people can cause real trouble. Once they have figured out that there is nothing to stop them from building a tower as high as they want, they may not be satisfied with their invasion of heaven. They may decide to exert their power horizontally as well as vertically, scouring the earth to see if there are other people in the world who can be made to speak their language and make their bricks for them. Preachers familiar with the strategies of colonialism will recognize the pattern.

By confusing the speech of the one-language people, God thwarts their ambitions—both the spiritual and the imperial kinds. What they most need, God decides, are some limits to their power, some dissenters in their midst. What they most need is not one language but many languages, not one name but many names. So God continues to create the world by creating a diversity of peoples who speak multiple languages, who use different words even when they seem to be pointing in the same direction: Hashem, Brahman, Holy Trinity, Allah. Are they speaking of the same thing or of different things? If different things, how so?

Henceforth, translation will become a necessary human activity. If people want their children to live in peace then they will have to put more effort into communicating with one another. They will have to figure out some way to share the world equitably with people who are no longer just like them.

Whether this is the moral of the story or the fallout from it, it highlights the way in which an old text can yield new meaning. It also sets the stage for all the encounters between strangers coming up in the first testament, both for good and for ill. On the "good" side are the three strangers who show up at Abraham and Sarah's tent one afternoon with a divine message for the old couple (Gen. 18:2). There is the stranger who wrestles with Jacob all night long, leaving him at dawn with a blessing and a limp (Gen. 32:24). These strangers do not have names, but plenty of others do.

One of the most mysterious strangers in the Abrahamic story cycle is named Melchizedek. He comes out of nowhere bearing bread and wine for Abram after a great battle (Gen. 14:17–20). The writer of Genesis identifies him as both king and priest, but since the Jewish priesthood is still hundreds of years in the future, Melchizedek is not that kind of priest. He is a priest of God Most High, and it is in the name of this God that he blesses Abram.

This is the first blessing Abram has received since God first came to him in Haran and promised to make a great nation of him. "I will bless those who bless you," God said on that occasion, "and the one who curses you I will curse; and in you all the families of the earth shall be blessed" (Gen. 12:3). Melchizedek is the first person to carry out God's will, in other words, though he and Abram do not worship at the same altar. After blessing Abram, Melchizedek blesses God. Then Abram gives him a tenth of everything, and Melchizedek vanishes back into his own narrative, leaving Abram to his.

The whole encounter takes only three verses, though you would never guess that from all the ink spent on Melchizedek in years to come. His name appears twice more in the Bible (at Psalm 110:4 and Hebrews 7:1–3), but that is nothing compared to Melchizedek's rich life *outside* the Bible, where his name shows up in the works of Philo and Josephus, in the Dead Sea Scrolls and Talmud, as well as in the writings of John Calvin, Martin Luther, and Joseph Smith. Even a brief survey of these sources suggests that what made Melchizedek so appealing to a wide array of writers was not how *much* they knew about him but how *little*, making him the perfect cipher for any point they wanted to win.

For some Jews, Melchizedek's blessing of Abram became the sign that God meant for Abraham's children to rule Jerusalem. For some Christians, Melchizedek provided a rationale for why the priesthood of Jesus superseded that of the Jews. What these and other approaches have in common is the way they use the ambiguities in the story to legitimize their own interests. They take Melchizedek's gracious blessing of Abram and turn it into an explanation for the superiority of their own blessedness before God.

Of course people are free to read their own theologies into the story. It is what people do. But as short as it is, the story already has a theology of its own, which is well attested in both testaments of Scripture: God works through religious strangers. From time to time, God sends the last people we would have expected to bless us and feed us. Some of them call God by the same name we do, and others do not. Some belong to priesthoods we recognize, and others do not. Some bless us in languages we understand, and others do not. In all these ways and more, God reminds us that we do not get to choose where our blessings come from. God will be the judge of that.

Preachers who wish to pursue this line of thought can easily come up with their own lists of inspired strangers: Jethro the priest of Midian, Ruth the faithful Moabite, Cyrus the Persian messiah, the magi from the east, the Syrophoenician woman, the Samaritan leper, several Roman centurions, the

Ethiopian eunuch—all of them religious strangers to the first hearers of these stories, all of them serving to advance the story of what God is doing with God's people, whether or not they are followers of Jesus.

This last point is worth repeating, since it is easy for interpreters of New Testament texts to assume that every healing encounter with Jesus or his disciples results in conversion. While this is clearly the point in some cases (most notably in stories from the Acts of the Apostles), it is less certain in stories from the synoptic Gospels.

When Jesus heals ten lepers in Luke 17 and only one—the Samaritan—returns to give thanks, Jesus says, "Get up and go on your way; your faith has made you well" (17:19). This response is notable for two reasons: first, because Jesus tells the leper to go on *his* way, not to come and follow Jesus; and second, because Jesus tells the leper that *his* faith has made him well. As natural as it may be for a Christian to assume that the leper's faith is his newfound faith in Jesus, that is not what the story says. It says that the tenth leper's *praise of God* is what sets him apart from the other nine. When the tenth leper thanks Jesus for healing him, Jesus has a moment very much like his moment with the Canaanite woman in Matthew 15. He is struck by a foreigner's great faith in God, which opens the way for him to act as God's anointed one. Afterward, both the Canaanite woman and the Samaritan leper go on their ways with no requirement that they begin calling God by another name.

This interpretation points to one of the most remarkable features of the monotheistic imagination, which is its commitment to honoring those beyond its bounds. The central texts of Judaism, Christianity, and Islam all make room for those who are not Jews, Christians, or Muslims. Whether these "religious others" are called strangers, aliens, foreigners, or People of the Book, they keep the monotheistic imagination alive to a God who is always greater—greater than our imaginations, greater than our God-given identities, greater than the religions that reveal God to us. By preserving the stories of faithful strangers, the Abrahamic faiths affirm that God is present with those who do not share our religion, race, or creed. This helps us meet what Sacks calls "the supreme religious challenge," which is "to see God's image in one who is not in our image."[6]

This, in short, may be the most important reason to honor the insights of other faith traditions in Christian sermons: because it is how we make room for God to be God. It is how we derail our attempts to make God in our own image. It is how we keep our imaginations alive to the sheep who do not belong to our fold, though they belong to God as well as we.

The Insights of Others

Preachers who have laid this groundwork have found different ways to incorporate the insights of other faith traditions in their sermons. Some have intentionally shifted their reading patterns so that references to writers from other traditions come naturally to mind when they are thinking through their sermons. Others have become explorers in their own neighborhoods, visiting different places of worship and seeking out relationships with members of different groups so that they have firsthand experience to report. Some take church members with them after a short course in receiving the hospitality of strangers. Yet others have formed or become members of interfaith groups in their communities or taken part in multifaith events or trips that have expanded their vocabulary along with their consciousness. In all these cases and more, the integrity of the preaching rests on the integrity of the preacher. One's life changes before one's preaching does.

If reading is the easiest place to begin, preachers have many options depending on their tastes. Fiction, poetry, and memoir can open doorways into other faith traditions that more academic works may not. For a sampler of short pieces from a wide variety of authors, read any volume in the *Best Spiritual Writing* series edited by Philip Zaleski.

If an academic approach is more to your liking, search the works of Martin Marty, Diana Eck, Stephen Prothero, or Eboo Patel for different views of religious pluralism in the United States. If you want to know at least as much as a student in your congregation who has taken a course in world religions, survey one of the introductory textbooks on the market.

Why do any of this if there are few people of other faiths in your community? Because the Christian imagination has always included people who are not physically present, for one thing. Because preaching is how you communicate with most of the people most of the time, for another. What you say from the pulpit establishes and reinforces the norms of public discourse in your congregation. How you speak of those who are not present constitutes Christian teaching about their worth before God. For the young people who are listening, your "posts" may affect how they make sense of all the other information they are getting from social networking sites about people of other (and no) faiths. For their elders, your sermons may clarify how relating to people of other faiths strengthens Christian witness instead of weakening it.

Different preachers will make different choices depending on their communal contexts and individual dispositions, but the preacher who never mentions the insights or presence of other religious traditions is making a clear choice, too.

Only You Know How

Since only you know how to answer the central question of this chapter in a way that makes sense for you and your congregation, other people's answers will be of limited use. Like any other decision you make about your preaching, this one will be rooted in your own wisdom and conviction about where the gospel is leading you and why. With that said, here are some general suggestions that may be helpful to consider.

Ground yourself in your own tradition. Whether you minister in the Catholic, Orthodox, or Protestant branch of Christ's body, know what your tradition says about engaging people of other faiths, both in belief and in practice. Make sure to look for recent resources, since many different kinds of Christians are rethinking their relationships with those who are not (and do not wish to become) Christian. If you are a Protestant serving a post-denominational church, create your own list of central biblical teachings on the subject and spend enough time with them to discover details you never noticed before. Develop a radical theology of hospitality. Ask God to guide you on this path.

Expand your frames of reference. Read and research as widely as you can. Actively seek friends of other faiths, in person or online. Look for opportunities to leave your comfort zone in the name of Christ, seeking God's image in those who are not in your image. The more you do any of these things, the better you will be able to speak of them in a natural way, without leaking fear or ignorance. At the same time, cultivate the virtue of theological humility, realizing that the only way to understand another person's religion is to practice it for a lifetime. Do unto others as you would have them do unto you.

Beware of spiritual shoplifting. When you come across something from another tradition that seems valuable, resist the temptation to Christianize it. Welcome it into your sermon as a friendly stranger who may guide you to something in your own tradition that you have overlooked or undervalued. After you have accurately reported an insight from another tradition—a Zen koan, a saying from the Hadith, a Jewish midrash—make the transition back to your own tradition by saying, "In the Christian view . . ." Whether you follow this phrase with admiration or calibration, it helps both you and your listeners register that there are different ways of conceiving reality, and they are not all the same.

Attend to the local news. While there may be times when it is necessary for you to weigh in on national or international news coverage, that is not your specialty. Your specialty is your "parish"—the geographical territory in which your congregants live—where national events have local consequences. What is going on with the zoning board? What new religious communities have applied for building permits in the last year and what response have they received? Who are the newest immigrants in town and how are things going for their children in the public schools? If you live in a "majority minority area" (where no cultural group has a majority), what is going on at soccer practice? Even if the answers to these questions are not as interesting to your listeners as the national news, they should be.

Preach the gospel that is good news for everyone. The Christian year includes a wide range of seasons. Some of them, like Christmas and Easter, focus more tightly on good news for Christians while others, like Epiphany and Pentecost, fling their seed more broadly. Whether or not you are a lectionary preacher, stay on the lookout for texts and teachings that might sound like good news to anyone, regardless of religious affiliation. By doing so, you may pique the interest of a visitor who thought Christian bread was only for Christians. Better yet, you may remind the loyal remnant that Jesus came for love of the whole world and is counting on the church to supply the salt and light.

Chapter 5

Discerning Authorities

TED A. SMITH

What kinds of authority are possible for preachers today? What is the theological significance of the changing nature of the authority of the preacher?

Thomas G. Long has always had a knack for discerning the questions of preachers—including those preachers who take his classes. In a 2010 interview he named what he described as a "major shift" in his students. "When I first started teaching," he said, "almost all of my students were eager and ready to be preachers—almost too eager and too ready to be preachers. . . ." Today, though, students tend to be "more reticent about that, less eager to assume authority, much more willing to postpone the assumption of authority, of being a pastor or a preacher. It's almost as if they are reverse images of the same problem, and that's the question of authority: Where do you get your authority, and how do you exercise your authority in the pulpit?"[1]

Long's students are right to ask these questions. Indeed, I would argue that no topic has been more significant in recent decades—both in the lived practice of preaching and in academic writing about preaching—than the topic of authority. Sometimes language of authority is right on top of our questions and conversations. Other times ideas about authority are buried deep within the topics we consciously discuss. One way or another, questions of authority are always with people who care about preaching these days. If it is obvious that being ordained and installed as the pastor of a congregation does not always secure a preacher's authority, it is not at all clear what kinds of authority *are* available to preachers. Perhaps even more deeply, it is not obvious that preachers should have anything like "authority" at all. Commitments to justice and equality have called the whole category of authority into question for preachers, congregants, and academics alike. It is little wonder that Long's students are tentative in claiming authority as preachers.

On questions of authority, many of them face not only a changing and complicated world outside themselves but also deep ambivalence within.

The Persistence of Authorities

Social theorists from many different camps have argued that authority has disappeared from the contemporary world. Such arguments have circulated for centuries, but they have been especially prominent in North Atlantic countries since the middle of the last century. French theorist Jean-François Lyotard, for instance, famously wrote about the end of the plausibility of what he called "metanarratives." Metanarratives organize snippets of sense and snapshots of experience into a history that has direction, meaning, and the power to authorize political formations. They can take many forms. They might tell how Jesus gave the keys to the kingdom of heaven to Peter, who handed them on to others through a long line of apostolic succession that grounds the authority of ordained leaders of the church today. Or they might tell a story about materialist dialectics propelling the human species from slave societies to feudalism to capitalism to socialism and finally to the enduring utopia of communism. Whatever the content of these metanarratives, Lyotard argues, they have ceased to be plausible in a postmodern age. And they have taken authority with them. For, as Lyotard asks, "Where, after the metanarratives, can legitimacy reside?"[2]

Many of those who cite Lyotard interpret the end of metanarratives as a good thing, the inauguration of a new era of freedom and multiplicity. Others tell the story of the disappearance of authority as something more like a tragedy. But both sides agree that authority has left our world.

It is worth noting the contradictions internal to these claims. After all, is there a narrative more "meta" than one about the end of all metanarratives? Exactly to the extent this narrative is plausible, it gives us reasons to reject it as true. Even when those who tell this story acknowledge exceptions, the framing of nonconforming realities as "exceptions" implies the presence of just the kind of strong, central direction to history that this story says is no longer plausible.

The contradictions within the story of the end of authority are compounded by the contradictions that appear in the acts of telling and hearing the story. For this story has been promulgated especially through channels that depend on some very established modes of authority. It often comes with the imprimatur of Europe, the distinction of "theory," and garlands of jargon. Many of its champions have been distinguished professors, conference speakers, and leaders of guilds. It has been proclaimed in named lectures and books with respected publishers. And these authorized modes of dissemination have been crucial for the hold this story has on our collective imaginations. The story of the end of authority has gained so much plausibility in part because authorized figures like Lyotard have told it. And the story returns the favor, for telling a powerful version of the story of the end of authority—whether the narrative takes the form of progress or decline—has packed pews, sold books, and fattened files for tenure and promotion. It has legitimated those who tell it, serving as a sign of sophistication and insight. The story of the end of authority has both depended on and fed modes of authority that are still very much alive.

These internal contradictions are compounded by more empirical failings to account for the enduring plurality of cultures in the United States. Many homileticians in black church traditions, for instance, have described the ongoing significance of authority for preachers. The subtitle of Samuel Proctor's book *The Certain Sound of the Trumpet* promises to help preachers craft "a sermon of authority."[3] In *The Sacred Art,* Olin Moyd describes the importance of a calling in the process of authorizing a person to preach. "The voice of the preacher becomes the voice of the Eternal," Moyd writes. "The audacious assignment is to speak for God and about God to the people of God of whom the preacher is just one called out as proclaimer."[4] Proctor and Moyd describe a world in which preachers still have the authority that comes from being called by God to speak for God.

Cleophus LaRue puts the point most sharply, making an explicit contrast between white and black homiletics on the matter of authority. LaRue does note that the authority of tradition is not what it once was. We are "living in a posttraditional age," he writes. And he stresses that African American readings of the Bible are "*nonmonolithic, multifaceted,* and *diverse.*" But LaRue also describes a culture in which some kinds of authority endure. "Blacks continue to attach great importance to the one who proclaims the message," LaRue writes. "Any ole individual will not do. The person up before them must have been called by God from the midst of the congregation to stand and proclaim the word of God. . . . Black preachers are still considered to be God's anointed, who bring to the waiting congregation the word from God."[5]

Preachers and homileticians like LaRue, Proctor, and Moyd describe black church cultures in which authority is still very much alive. One could argue that there are many black church cultures—and even more modes of African American religious life—and that LaRue, Proctor, and Moyd describe only one part of a much larger and more complex whole. Perhaps the authority of God's anointed is less powerful in some circles. Perhaps it is less persuasive to younger generations. But naming some counter-examples to these counter-examples would not restore a grand narrative about the end of authority. It would rather push us to look more carefully at the particularities of local situations so that we can see the kinds of authority that might or might not be at work. It would push us away from all-encompassing narratives and toward smaller-scale studies that were both more modest and more grounded in empirical observation. And it would push us away from sweeping stories of progress or decline and toward more nuanced, grounded evaluations of the ways authority actually operates—or fails to operate—in particular contexts.

Neither Persuasion nor Coercion

Turning our attention to the different ways authority plays out in different situations might mean that we should forego sweeping generalizations. But it does not mean that we should try to proceed without concepts. On the contrary, our attempts at understanding the lived complexity of social interactions could be helped by a more precise concept of authority. As that concept gains precision and particularity it will necessarily cease to describe the full diversity of phenomena across centuries and cultures. But even (or especially) as it fails to account for the myriad particularities of lived experience, a well-formed concept can be illuminating.

We stand in particular need of a concept of authority that can help us frame moral questions without determining the answers to them in advance. "Authority" can be such a charged word that it short-circuits our thinking. We treasure it or loathe it or just want to get away from it. What we need is a concept that can help us *understand* it. For understanding will be required for wise judgment in particular situations.

The political philosopher Hannah Arendt offers one good candidate for such a concept in her 1954 essay "What Is Authority?" Arendt does not define authority in the abstract. She rather describes a particular kind of authority that arose through long successions of dominant cultures in Western Europe. In Arendt's narrative, Greek philosophy contributed a metaphysics that stressed the absolute qualities of truths that transcended prevailing beliefs. The Romans seized on this structure of transcendent truth and joined it to their own practice of venerating the founders of a tradition and authorizing those who kept faith with them by extending the tradition in later eras. After the fall of the Roman Empire, this tight amalgamation of religion, tradition, and authority passed into the Catholic Church. In Arendt's telling, this very particular combination came to define what authority meant in Latin

Christendom and its cultural descendants. Authority could be passed to different institutions. It could authorize very different values, institutions, and leaders. But it retained this basic structure over the centuries. Now, Arendt writes, authority has all but disappeared.[6]

Arendt's story about authority claims too much. It misses the places where something like the authority she describes still exists, sometimes not just holding on but gaining strength. And it misses the ways in which other modes of authority have risen to prominence in different eras and different cultures. But Arendt's story can still do a lot to help us develop a useful concept of authority. Arendt's concept of authority has the advantage of a self-conscious rootedness in particular historical events. It can acknowledge its own historical particularity. Even in its particularity, though, this concept can define a more general category in the ways that a useful concept does. It can do this work because of the dominance that this particular kind of authority achieved in Latin Christendom. I would lament this domination and resist the legacies of the violence that established it. But lamentation and resistance do not deny its power to define a shared social sense of what counts as "authority." Arendt is right that the power of this particular species of authority has eroded. But it has a kind of afterlife, for it has created a social space that can be filled by other combinations of beliefs, practices, and institutions. The very particular kind of authority that Arendt describes is like a mollusk that has vacated a shell that can be inhabited by other creatures. That shell might even be lifted to an ear in play or turned into jewelry. Many different modes of authority compete for that space now. Even if none of those newcomers can make the shell of authority into a permanent home, it still defines a sense of what we are missing. And so the shape of that left-behind space matters.

The defining feature of the shape of this authority, in Arendt's view, is that it involves something other than persuasion, on the one hand, and violent coercion, on the other. Unlike rational persuasion, a statement with authority does not just call on the beliefs and interests that a person already knows she has. Authority does not depend on these conscious beliefs and interests; it rather grounds and transforms them. Thus an authoritative argument can convince even when it cannot persuade.

More controversially, Arendt argues that authority offers something more and other than mere coercion. A truly authoritative claim can win assent without threats of punishment or promises of reward. It calls instead on our sense of what we *ought* to do. And that sense of obligation cannot be reduced to mere coercion. This is the difference between authority and tyranny, as Arendt sees them. Authority sustains the kind of shared beliefs that give rise to community and make social action possible. Tyranny, on the other hand, arises when authority breaks down, leaving nothing that can resolve disputes or bind a community together except force. Tyranny uses some kind of violence to limit freedom and force compliance. Authority, as Arendt defines it, is "an obedience in which [people] retain their freedom."[7]

In the dense tangles of daily life, authority and tyranny are often bound more tightly together than Arendt's definitions suggest. Even when authority operates without force in the present moment, it often depends on past violence that established it as authoritative. But even when these tangles of violence and authority are acknowledged, Arendt's analysis can help us identify a *promise* inherent in any set of relationships that would stake its claim to the shell of authority: a promise to be something other than mere coercion. And that promise establishes a standard by which we can judge different modes of authority. We can evaluate them by the degree to which they do in fact change minds, shape imaginations, and create communities with a power that transcends coercion.

Informed by Arendt's concept of an authority that promises to be something better than violence in its Sunday best, but delivered from her assumption that authority can take only one form and her story about the disappearance of authority from the world, we can begin to discern multiple modes of authority at work over the centuries and in our own time. Seeing these diverse modes of authority lets us begin to tell richer and more particular stories about the movements of authority in different preaching contexts. And refusing to reject authority in advance as nothing more than mere coercion makes possible more subtle evaluations of the ways these different modes of authority function.

The Authority of Office

Significant shifts in authority have been happening. Arendt was right about this in 1954, and the changes have only accelerated in the decades that followed. But the best way to understand these changes is not through a single story about the disappearance of authority. It is through many smaller stories about the erosion of some kinds of authority and the rise of others. Many preaching contexts, for instance, have seen a decline in what I will call the authority of office. At the same time they have seen the gathering power of an authority of authenticity that sometimes displaces the authority of office but more often operates alongside it in ways that undermine it, enhance it, or otherwise transform it.[8]

The authority of office arises when a trusted institution designates a person to speak or act for it in some capacity. The authority of the institution then flows to the individual officeholder. The authority of office is at work when the authority of the nation flows to the president, the authority of the school flows to the teacher, or the authority of the church flows to one it has ordained. This flow depends first of all on the prior authority of the institution. A strong institution has a deep well of authority that it can draw on and distribute to the people that it designates. A strong nation, for instance, bestows such authority on the office of the president that people show the president respect even when they dislike the person or disagree with particular policies. The authority of office also depends on a shared sense that a person has come to hold the office in the right way. If an election is disputed, for instance, a president might have less authority even if the nation itself retains the trust, affection, and commitment of its citizens.

These crucial moves sustaining the authority of office are performed and performed again in many different ways. Authority is not just an idea in our heads. It is something we do together. It is public, social, embodied, and enacted. Churches tend to mark the transfer of authority to officehold- ers through formal rituals of inauguration, ordination, or installation. Echoes of these rituals resound long after their initial performance. When we use titles like "Reverend" or "Bishop" without irony, for instance, we remem- ber and reaffirm the church's bestowal of authority on some individual. This bestowal can be made visible through distinctive clerical attire like robes, mitres, chasubles, and stoles. It can be performed through movement into spaces reserved for clergy, like the space behind a pulpit or a table. It can also be performed more subtly, as when a person moves her body or speaks in ways that a congregation regards as typical of the holder of an office. There are as many ways to perform the authority of office as there are offices to hold and people to hold them. But all these performances remember and renew the authority of the institution and the sharing of that authority with the officeholder.

The authority of office has been crucial for preachers of many different traditions over the centuries. It is the mode of authority that most closely resembles the mode that gave rise to Hannah's Arendt's concept of authority. It has had great power. And it has long been contested. When Pennsylvania Presbyterian Gilbert Tennent railed against "The danger of an unconverted ministry" in 1740, he denounced ordained and installed clergy as "Orthodox, Letter-learned, regular Pharisees," for they had not undergone true conver- sion. That conversion—not ordination by a church that had lost its way— should be the real source of authority, Tennent argued.[9]

Long-standing challenges to the authority of office have intensified in recent decades, and most stories about the decline of authority are more precisely stories about the decline of the authority of office. Fred Craddock discerned these movements in the wake of the cultural changes that are usually gathered under the sign of "The Sixties." Craddock argues in *As One without Authority* that "It is generally recognized that many blows struck against the pulpit come not because of its peculiar faults but because it is part of a traditional and entrenched institution, and all such institutions—religious, political, or otherwise—are being called into question."[10] When institutions are called into question, they cannot transfer authority as readily to their officeholders. And the decline in the authority of office can be felt not just in a vague sense that preachers do not command the respect they once did but also in very material declines in pay relative to other kinds of work.

This phenomenon is not universal. As I argued above, Samuel Proctor, Olin Moyd, and Cleophus LaRue have stressed the ways that authority endures for many preachers in black church traditions. This authority draws from many sources, but the authority of office is important in the mix. The authority of office retains at least some power across a wide variety of traditions. It operates wherever a formal title indicates respect or some article of clothing marks a person as called from the wider community to a particular form of service. It operates everywhere that ordination matters.

The sharpest critics of authority have often had the authority of office in mind when they have denounced authority in more general terms. And the authority of office has deserved the sharpest criticism that we can muster. It has been enacted in ways that exclude from office not just some individuals but whole classes of faithful, gifted, baptized Christians. It has propped up little tyrants who rule over their congregations in ways that stroke their egos and enrich their bank accounts. The authority of office has contributed to closed networks of officeholders who have shielded one another—and the institutions that are the source of their authority—from scrutiny, enabling the sexual abuse of children and other horrors.

The authority of office has also sustained generous leaders who have lifted up whole communities. It has empowered prophetic speech that congregations might not have wanted to hear—speech that had to do something more radical than persuade people on the basis of beliefs they already had, speech that required *authority*. And healthy institutions can regulate the authority of office in ways that other modes of authority—like the mode sociologist Max Weber called "charismatic"—cannot be regulated. Institutions can establish and follow procedures that ensure transparency, review, and accountability. They can remove people from office for abuses of authority. They can set limits to the boundaries of authority, making clear that it extends to some spheres but not others. The officeholder then is not set apart in an absolute way, as a different kind of being who has authority in every situation, but in a more modest and functional way, as one member of a community who performs a particular role on behalf of that community. Thomas Long advocates something like this limited authority of office when he describes the way a preacher comes from the wider assembly into a new position in relation to those who are gathered. This "new position of the preacher is not so much a change in status," Long writes, "but a change in place and function." Preachers with this kind of authority are not necessarily wiser or more holy than other members of the assembly, according to Long. They are not authorized to exercise authority in every aspect of life. But they do have the limited, real authority that comes with ordination, what Long calls "the authority of being identified by the faithful community as the one called to preach and the one who has been prayerfully set apart for this ministry."[11] They have the limited authority proper to an office.

Institutions can even establish policies that ensure that the authority of office will be open to more people than a community might authorize through less formal means. Indeed, one of the most important developments in recent decades is the shift that has happened as some Christian denominations have made the authority of office at least formally available to women and to gay and lesbian people. Rules around ordination have long excluded women and people who identified as lesbian or gay. The authority of office, then, has been a significant barrier to equality. It remains so for the vast majority of Christians in the United States today. But a handful of denominations have changed their rules to open ordination to people without regard to gender or sexual orientation. Significant—even massive—informal barriers remain in place, even in these denominations. But it matters that the rules governing the authority of office have changed. And now the authority of office is sometimes the greatest source of authority available to a person who faces discrimination from many other sources. Some of the savviest female, gay, and lesbian pastors I know wear clerical collars in some situations for just this reason. The authority of office creates at least limited and temporary hierarchies. But in the lived complexity of the real world, it can also be a force for equality.

The Authority of Authenticity

Where the authority of office has waned, other modes of authority have grown in power. They have often presented themselves as alternatives to the authority of office, as in Gilbert Tennent's call for a recognition of the authority that comes from conversion. And sometimes these different modes have upended older modes and made authority accessible to a completely new set of people. But most of the time they have not displaced the authority of office so much as arisen alongside it to check, supplement, and transform it. One of the most important of these increasingly influential modes is the authority of authenticity.

Talk of "authenticity" seems to be everywhere these days. A study of several hundred listeners to sermons found that they prized a delivery with *"intense authenticity."*[12] One leadership consultant stresses that it is especially important to "make it real" and "authentic" when preaching to young adults.[13] Other authors underscore the need to be "authentic and transparent," for "preaching is not just about what you say; it's very much about who you are."[14] This emphasis on "keeping it real" cuts across many cultural groups and denominations, playing an important role even in traditions that still value the authority of office. Authenticity has become a sign of our times.

Academic homileticians have stressed especially the egalitarian and emancipatory potential of authorities of authenticity. In *Weaving the Sermon,* pioneering feminist homiletician Christine M. Smith expresses grave concerns about the ways authority sets some apart from others. Her concerns about hierarchy are so great that she questions "the very term *authority* and its appropriateness for a description of women's preaching." But as she develops her vision for women's preaching she does not leave authority completely behind. Instead she stresses the need to create a different kind of authority, one built on mutuality, relationship . . . and authenticity. "The mark of authenticity and women's authority," she writes, "is deep connection to one's self, to God, and to others." Authority comes when "intimacy and authenticity work together." The best reading of Smith would take seriously her reframing of authority. She does not end up rejecting every kind of authority. Instead she calls for a shift from an authority of office or tradition to an authority of mutuality and authenticity.[15]

Anna Carter Florence makes related moves in developing a vision of preaching as testimony. Florence names with great clarity a shift from an authority of office to an authority of authenticity. "More and more," she writes,

> preachers are relying not on outside authorities as the proof of their words (that is, ecclesial bodies that make decisions about leadership or orthodoxy), but on the authority of testimony: preaching what they have seen and heard in the biblical text, and what they believe about it. More and more, preachers are finding that what makes their sermons authoritative for

their people is not the number of footnotes but the depth of the preacher's engagement with the Scriptures and life itself.[16]

Florence calls preachers to speak the truth that is theirs to tell. "God's people do not hold back *anything*," she writes, "not ferocious love or ferocious grief." What matters for testimony is not that a person holds an office or displays the training that is a requirement for holding that office but that she speaks from the heart.[17]

Speaking from the heart can become not just expressive but authoritative in a culture that values the individual self as a site of divine revelation and perhaps even sacred in and of itself. When the self—not some tradition or institution—is taken to be ultimate, or the site of connection to whatever is ultimate, then testimony from and about that self carries the strongest form of authorization. Because authority is always a collaborative social event, if testimony is to be authoritative, it is not enough for a preacher to *be* authentic. The preacher must *display* authenticity in ways that can be received as such. Because the real self is taken to be the ground of authority, performances of authenticity must find ways to display to others what they will see as one's real self. And in Western cultures that define the real self in contrast to every public role, the real self is taken to be the self we are in our private life. Thus the authority of authenticity depends on a speaker's ability to present a private self in public.

Preachers, politicians, and others present private selves in public by refusing the trappings of office for markers of private life. They might give up a clerical robe for a Hawaiian shirt. They might replace formal oratory with a more conversational style. They might leave behind polished speech for a manner of speaking in which the voice crests, stumbles, and even breaks as it does when a person is overcome with strong feelings. They will stress eye contact more than ever. They might give up carefully crafted manuscripts for an extemporaneous style that does more to suggest that they are speaking from the heart. They might replace studied gestures with the kinds of movements one makes in casual and conversational settings. It can be all the better if these gestures seem a little awkward or idiosyncratic. The kinds of movements that a class devoted to cultivating the authority of office would seek to iron out of a preacher can become significant resources for a preacher who would make use of the authority of authenticity.

Christine Smith and Anna Carter Florence both rightly stress the egalitarian potential of this kind of authority. Because one does not need the permission of any institution to speak in these ways, all kinds of people—even people institutions refuse to authorize—can testify with the authority of authenticity. Florence notes the resource this kind of authority has been for women denied the authority of office. Anne Hutchinson, Sarah Osborn, and Jarena Lee faced some situations where they were not allowed to preach. But they could *testify*. And they could do so with the authority of authenticity.

The authority of authenticity has done much to open up new possibilities for long-marginalized groups. But it also deserves scrutiny. It can be learned, and so it can be faked. Consultants now offer to help train business leaders in displaying their authenticity. And history is full of expert performances in which a raspy voice, a tear rolling down the cheek, and the most heartfelt eye-contact disguise what can only be called lies. The authority of authenticity can also be yoked to populist but antidemocratic politics. For instance, in the Republican primaries for the 2016 presidential election, Donald Trump presented himself as an outsider, untainted by the authority of office. He grounded his authority instead in his willingness to "be real" and to say "what everyone was thinking but no one else would say." When those who supported him were asked about his appeal, they repeatedly stressed that he was "authentic."[18]

It is not just that the authority of authenticity can empower individuals who advocate antidemocratic policies. It is that this mode of authority is difficult to hold accountable within any system of oversight or checks and balances. The authority of office can be regulated by procedures because its power derives in part from a sense that right procedures have been followed. But the authority of authenticity derives part of its power from its ability to set itself against procedures and institutions. Attempts to curtail it can have the effect of adding to its power.

The authority of authenticity seems to be equally available to all people. After all, no one needs anyone's permission to keep it real. But in practice it can be more difficult for some groups of people to display authenticity in ways that give them public authority. Authentic testimony always runs the risk of remaining private in its significance. Hearers can receive testimony respectfully as the truthful expression of a real self and then dismiss it to the purgatory of merely private status. "That's your view," a hearer can say, "and I respect it as your view. You have a right to hold it. But no one else is obliged to be moved by it." In these cases testimony can be authentic without being authoritative.

Testimony can make the quantum leap to public authority when it is joined to a public persona—perhaps defined by an office like president or pastor—that is already engaged in a wide web of relationships and institutions.[19] Then the performance of authenticity requires giving listeners the ability to see the harmony between this public persona and a private and seemingly more real persona. The presence of the true and private self can charge the public role with new authority, as when President Bill Clinton's voice grew raspy as he made unbroken eye contact with the camera and told citizens that he felt their pain. That kind of performance requires that a speaker step outside a public role for a short time. It requires the ability to take that public role for granted, to know that one can leave it aside in one moment and return to it in the next.[20] It is much easier for a speaker to take a public role for granted when the public is already disposed to grant a speaker that role. And publics are often more ready to grant that privilege when the speaker looks and sounds like the kind of person they already think *should* occupy that role. Women and members of underrepresented groups of many kinds often cannot take their public roles for granted in this way.

Consider a recent example from national politics. In 2010 an explosion on the offshore oil rig *Deepwater Horizon* killed eleven crew members, sank the rig, and left an open wound on the sea floor that sent more than 200 million barrels of oil gushing into the Gulf of Mexico. President Barack Obama addressed the nation, making credible promises to hold accountable the people and corporations that were responsible. But many observers wanted him to show more *anger* at the spill. They did not have a problem with his policies. They criticized his affect. He seemed too cool, too detached. He did not seem authentically angry in the way that George W. Bush did after the attacks of September 11, 2001.[21] But if Obama had shown this kind of anger in public, he would have run the risk of ceasing to seem "presidential" and starting to seem like an "angry black man"—a trope that racism has infused with so much cultural power that it can exert a gravitational pull that draws otherwise ordinary actions under its sign. Obama could not take his public persona for granted in the way that Bush could. And that made it harder for him to project authenticity.

The mere fact of *being* authentic may be equally available to all. But drawing *authority* from authenticity is often easier for people whose identities line up with the identities that a public already associates with particular public roles. And so the authority of authenticity can end up reproducing existing structures of power.

The authority of authenticity can also take a toll on the one who makes use of it. Acting authentically can be liberating. But translating authentic action into a source of authority is risky business. When authenticity becomes a resource for pastoral authority, the pastor begins to use his or her "true" self in instrumental ways. The stuff of private life—relationships, feelings, leisure activities, and more—all get turned into resources that can be displayed to enhance authority and effectiveness. This act of instrumental display transforms the stuff of private life. Like the touch of Midas, the authority of authenticity can drain the life from private life even as it turns it into political gold.

Sociologist Arlie Russell Hochschild describes effects like these in a study of flight attendants who are trained not just to offer good service but to really, truly care about customers and to display the authenticity of their care to customers. Hochschild compares this "emotional labor" to method acting's emphasis on authentic expression. And she notes the problems that it causes for the attendants. Forming their emotions for public display leaves them feeling empty and alienated from their own feelings. Many of them struggle in personal relationships even when they thrive in displaying authentic care on the plane.[22]

Instrumentalizing authenticity can contribute to such problems not only for people in caregiving roles but also for people in leadership roles. The political philosopher Michael Ignatieff experienced some of these difficulties when he decided to run for office in his native Canada. In a memoir he describes the challenges of maintaining any meaningful private self in the course of a campaign that required not just that he offer winning policies but that he display an authentic self that voters could relate to and enjoy. This performance came with a cost. "As you submit to the compromises demanded by public life," he writes, "your public self begins to alter the person inside." He describes feeling as if some evil twin had taken over his life. He felt as if something inside him had died. He worried that he had become nothing more than the "fixed rictus" of the smile that politics demanded. "Looking back now," he writes, "I would say that some sense of hollowness, some sense of a divide between the face you present to the world and the face you reserve for the mirror, is a mark of sound mental health."[23]

Preachers face both the challenges that Hochschild names for caregivers and those that Ignatieff names for leaders. The two describe an irony that many preachers know all too well: displays of authenticity for the sake of authority can compromise the health and vitality of the feelings, thoughts, and relationships that are displayed—especially when they are real.

In naming these risks to the authority of authenticity, I do not mean to argue that it is less just or more problematic than the authority of office. The authority of office has plenty of perils of its own. As its critics point out, it is exclusive, almost by its nature. It, too, can be faked. Forged credentials are as fraudulent as crocodile tears. And the authority of office invites hypocrisy and the alienation and self-loathing that accompany it—exactly the problems that those who prize authenticity want to overcome. Both modes of authority have some promise, and each mode has problems that are proper to it. The ratios of promise and problems will depend on individual lives and contexts. And so the story of authority's shift away from office and toward authenticity should be told neither as a narrative of progress nor as a narrative of decline. It should rather be told as a story that individual preachers can use to illumine their own contexts in ways that help them respond with wisdom, integrity, and faithfulness.

Discernment

Significant changes in beliefs, practices, and institutions have made for significant changes in the ways authority functions today. The best way to understand these changes is not as a single shift from the establishment of authority to the absence of authority but as a complex tangle of shifts in the powers of different kinds of authority. A shift from the authority of office to the authority of authenticity names one significant strand in that tangle of changes. There are other kinds of authority beyond these two. We might also look for contemporary forms of charismatic authority, the kind of authority that clients loan to life coaches and personal trainers, the kind of authority that can be generated by a democratic process, and more.[24] The balance of power between these many sources of authority is moving in more than one direction. But a focused story about one shift from office to authenticity can help many preachers make sense of what is happening in their contexts, even if what is happening is different from what the story describes.

Seeing the multiple kinds of authority suggests that many arguments against authority are really arguments against one kind of authority and, perhaps implicitly, arguments *for* another kind of authority. And seeing the promises and problems of each kind of authority suggests that what we should be seeking is not some single, right kind of authority but the most just and faithful ways to engage the kinds of authority that are at work in our own contexts. Wise pastors will see what resources are available, think critically about them, and reflect with honesty on the means and effects of their own relationships to these authorities. There is no simple and exclusive divine authorization of one kind of authority over all the others. But this does not mean that theology is irrelevant to questions of authority. It rather means that theology will be done, as always when it is done best, in the hustle and flow of everyday life.

PART III

Changing
Congregational Contexts

Chapter 6

Preaching in Multicultural Congregations

A Round-Table Discussion

LEONORA TUBBS TISDALE, EDITOR

How do we preach to faith communities that are highly diverse in terms of race, ethnicity, class, theological background, sexual orientation, and more?

Authors:

Jin S. Kim, Pastor, Church of All Nations, Minneapolis, Minnesota, and founder of Underground Seminary

Jacqueline J. Lewis, Pastor, Middle Collegiate Church, New York City, and Executive Director of The Middle Project, New York

Gabriel Salguero, Pastor, The Lamb's Church, New York City, and President of the National Latino Evangelical Coalition (*editor's note*: He is now serving as pastor of Iglesia El Calvario, a multiethnic church in Orlando, Florida)

Nibs Stroupe, Pastor, Oakhurst Presbyterian Church, Decatur, Georgia

Editor's Note: In this chapter I asked four pastors of multicultural congregations to reflect on the challenges of preaching in their contexts and to share what they have learned by doing so. I then compiled their responses, listing them in alphabetical order, and put them together in roundtable format. After compiling the responses, I gave the authors an opportunity to rework or add to their comments in response to one another.

1) Tell us about the makeup of your congregation. To whom are you preaching in a typical worship service (in terms of race, ethnicity, class, theological background, age, sexual orientations, educational background, etc.)?

JIN S. KIM: Our congregation is diverse in many ways. Church of All Nations was founded in 2004 by mostly second-generation Korean American Presbyterians. A dozen years later we are made up of immigrants from every continent, Euro-Americans, African Americans, and a few Native Americans.

Many mixed race couples and multicultural families find our church attractive, and in the past two years we have become a majority white (of largely Scandinavian heritage) congregation. We span all generations from newborns to ninety-year-olds, but two-thirds of our members are between twenty and forty years of age. Generationally, we are predominantly millennial.

JACQUI LEWIS: Middle Collegiate Church in Manhattan is a welcoming, artistic, inclusive congregation of about 975 members who are called by God boldly to do a new thing on the earth. That new thing, we believe, is to rehearse the Reign of God on earth right here and now. On any given Sunday, I stand at the pulpit and look out at what seems to me the most incredible diversity. There is a mom with strawberry blonde hair who grew up in Louisiana. She is an accomplished executive and is always rocking out to the gospel music with her two sons, ages one and five. Over there is a white straight couple, actors, who adopted three children from Ethiopia. There is a biracial woman who will retire next year. She identifies as African American, and the racial strife in America is breaking her heart. There is a black straight couple with two boys, one an athlete and the other a singer. There is a Chinese lesbian who works in law enforcement. She helped us to establish a Lunar New Year celebration, in which a fabulous Chinese family with a mom, a dad, and three stunningly brilliant children always participate. There is a Latina who works for a large New York company who is wondering if she should propose to the woman she loves.

We are black, white, Asian, Hispanic. We are gay, lesbian, straight, bisexual, and transgender. Some of us own many houses, some of us live in SROs (single room occupancies). Most of us struggle to live in a city that is so expensive. All of us are committed to creating a more just society. We walk by the so-called black church or Chinese church or gay church to come to Middle Church, where everyone is welcome just as they are when they come through the door.

We are mostly baby boomers, but our fastest growing demographic is millennials. Ten years ago we had about ten, and now we have about 150. Middle Church and the Middle Project commissioned a study by Robert P. Jones of Public Religion Research, and the findings helped us to focus on raising millennial leaders. They lead justice projects, plan worship, sing in our choir, and comprise half of our board.

GABRIEL SALGUERO: The Lamb's Church is a multicultural, multiethnic, multiclass evangelical church located on the Lower East Side of Manhattan. This section of Manhattan, also known as LoHo or LES, is near

Chinatown and Little Italy. Its boundaries stretch from Houston to Delancey Streets between the Bowery and the East River. This area once housed African Americans freed from slavery, immigrants from Ireland during the potato famines, Jews, Germans, Southern Italians, and many more seeking better lives for their families. The motto of the LES can be read on the welcome signs throughout: "Welcome to the Lower East Side . . . where cultures mingle."

The Lamb's Church is a trilingual congregation with two services. Our 10:00 a.m. service is in Mandarin, and our noon worship service is bilingual, in English and Spanish. Every three months, and on Easter, Christmas, Thanksgiving, and New Year's Day, we have a joint worship gathering in all three languages. The congregation is made up of first-generation Latino and Chinese immigrants, many of whom are in their sixties and seventies, as well as U.S.-born Hispanics and Chinese parishioners who are in their twenties and thirties. In addition, one-third of the congregation is made up of a mixture of English-only speaking whites, West-Indians, Filipinos, Latinos, Africans, and African Americans. This group tends to be between twenty-five and forty years of age. We often refer to the Lamb's Church as a motley crew.

Besides the linguistic barriers the biggest challenges are the class and educational differences in the congregation. We have many younger parishioners who have college and graduate degrees. Many of the first-generation Hispanics are working-class men and women with a high-school education or less. A number are also undocumented immigrants. The first-generation Chinese immigrants have a mixed educational background from high school to graduate degrees, mostly from China. Ninety percent of these members speak predominantly Mandarin or Cantonese. Most of the U.S.-born or 1.5-generation Chinese members speak English and Mandarin.

NIBS STROUPE: Oakhurst Presbyterian is a church in the city. Although we are technically located in the small town of Decatur, Georgia, we are part of the greater Atlanta area. Because we are a church in the city, we have seen our context change dramatically at least twice. Once we were all of one kind—almost nine hundred Anglo members, reduced to about eighty members over a period of fifteen years, as the white members fled the neighborhood when African Americans moved in. They moved in because their housing had been taken and torn down by the city of Atlanta in order to build sports arenas. That story continues in many ways in many American cities today. Oakhurst decided to stay in its neighborhood, and through powerful and tenacious leadership by its elders and ministers, it has not only survived but is currently thriving, even as the neighborhood again changes with gentrification taking place.

Because of our church's connection to race through its history, the power of race remains a central theme of our life together. Though we emphasize many other issues, it is always race that brings us back to our context of seeking to be the people of God. The racial categories of our membership are barely majority Anglo, with 40 percent African American, a few Latino and Asian members, and a growing number of multiracial members. We are mostly middle class, though there continue to be a number of our members who live in grinding poverty. In 1991 we decided to openly welcome gay and lesbian persons as full members, so we have a number of people who bring that perspective to our life together. There are several seminaries and universities in the Atlanta area, and because of that reality, over 10 percent of our members have their doctorates. We now have just over four hundred members, and in the families of our members, we have more than one hundred children participating in the life of the church.

2) What are the expectations of the varied members of your congregation regarding what a sermon should be and do? Where are those expectations similar and where do they differ? How do you as a preacher navigate the differences?

JIN S. KIM: The preaching moment is for us an exploration of the contours of contemporary Christian community and how we might live into our common vocation of creating and expanding the beloved community. I have learned that our people are more informed by the countenance and character of the preacher than by the art of delivery. More than anything they want to know that I am fully attentive to reading the people, the Word, and the world, and their integral interrelation. Before I expound on the wisdom of the ages, do I know who I am? Do I acknowledge my own limitations matter-of-factly, so that all of us can be okay with our real selves? How much of what I believe is gospel truth and how much cultural assumptions?

We have found, mostly through the school of hard knocks, that different generations and cultures tend to feel comforted by different characteristics of God. Speaking deeply to one culture may not resonate in another. Difference requires us to grow in forbearance.

The challenge of multicultural worship is that nothing one does resonates with everyone. A sermon illustration that touches one group may inadvertently be offensive to another. No one musical genre satisfies the whole. Yet we have all experienced the wonder of rich togetherness precisely because this seeming cacophony of voices could only sound like harmony by the grace of God. Sometimes congregation members flatly disagree with my biblical interpretation. Mostly, we've been a church with a big heart and try to be flexible in nonessential matters. Lucky for me, our people have over the years developed a consensus on what is essential and what is not. We understand that even though the Bible is God's eternal word to us, all theology is provisional. "Hang on to Jesus and let it be," one might say.

One way that we get beyond theological and ecclesiological differences is in the sharing of testimony, a practice that we explicitly credit to the African American church. Our members share their testimony in cell groups, meetings of every kind, and especially in our worship service. Congregants are welcome to share their whole lives, including their struggles and shame. Twice a year, at Pentecost and Thanksgiving, we have an open microphone where anyone can come forward and share. At other times, a member may share a more involved testimony in place of the sermon.

I serve as senior pastor with a large, diverse staff, yet for years I have preached about half the Sundays per year. Sharing the pulpit with "regular folk" means that we hear from many of us, not just a few. This is our way of living into the priesthood of all believers. The sermon is always addressed to "us" and thus is never a private spirituality lesson.

JACQUI LEWIS: This community expects our clergy—diverse in theology, ethnicity, sexual orientation, and gender—to preach a vision of a preferred reality. They expect us to "story" for them what God is doing in the world and how we can take part in that, how we can partner with God to change the story. They expect to be inspired. They expect the sermon to move them, to make them feel deeply. They want to laugh and cry. They want to be taught and challenged. They can't always describe the ineffable, but they want to encounter the Holy intimately. They think of the whole worship celebration, as do I, as the sermon. But they want the preached word to meet them where they are and move them closer to God and to creation. They want the word to heal them so that they can heal the world. A few want to be told they are sinners, but only a very few—like five. A few want to hear that Jesus is the way, the truth, and the life—and I mean only ten. Most want to hear of a God who is welcoming enough for all of our crazy diversity, and if that is true, they want to know that God will welcome the strangeness of other strangers.

We celebrate not only Lunar New Year but also Asian History Month, Black History Month, and Hispanic Heritage Month. At Pentecost we celebrate all of our many tribes and nations as we praise God in one voice. We pray the Lord's Prayer every Sunday in the language and version of our choice. It is a Pentecost moment every week.

Our little children lead us by singing in worship and serving communion. When twenty of them sit by the pulpit during the message for all ages, when the happy gurgles and "I am hungry" cries rise up from our babies, we feel alive and like the Reign of God is on its way.

Music and the arts are languages that transcend our diversity and bind us together. All kinds of dance, puppet shows, drama, poetry, and visual arts show up in worship every week. Music of all genres—from Bach to Beatles to spirituals to sacred anthems to jazz and blues—are used to inspire and challenge us to heal our souls and heal the world.

GABRIEL SALGUERO: Although we self-identify as an evangelical Nazarene congregation, many of our Generation Xers and millennials have very little reference for our particular church traditions and history. Many of them did not grow up in church and have little knowledge of differences between Reformed and Wesleyan thought. Some of our more seasoned members are very well aware of the distinctions and want to make sure I highlight them in my preaching and teaching. In short, the expectations can be very varied. Some listeners want affirmation of the convictions they hold most dear while others want to hear what the gospel has to say for a new generation. Many of the younger members tend to be biblically illiterate and unfamiliar with the gospel.

In addition, the expectations vary in terms of delivery style. Some of our parishioners prefer a delivery style that is more poetic and in keeping with African American and Hispanic preaching, such as is highlighted in Evans Crawford's book *The Hum*.[1] Others prefer more prose and didactic preaching, often referred to as "three points and a poem." It is as if some listeners want a TED talk while others want a revival sermon. Among many of our older immigrant congregants, a forty-minute sermon is customary. Among many of the younger or newer members, twenty minutes is the threshold. The gospel can come to us in a variety of formats, but preparation and delivery are quite different for each.

As a pastor, I have the advantage of preaching fifty-two weeks a year. This allows me to use a variety of styles of engagement and delivery. I continuously draw from classic sources and readings from different cultures while also pulling from more contemporary sources from the Internet, media, and popular culture. To speak to this multiplicity of demands, I have developed a hybridity of preaching. My sermons are not only multilingual but also intentionally mixed in delivery styles and sermon sources. Hybrid preaching or "jazz-preaching," as I call this style, infuses both tradition and innovation. The advice from L. Gregory Jones to implement "traditioned innovation"[2] is also appropriate for me as a preacher. Or perhaps more fitting are the words of Jesus, "Every scribe who has been trained for the kingdom of heaven is like the master of a household who brings out of his treasure what is new and what is old" (Matt. 13:52). Preaching requires a dialectic that is both/and, not either/or.

Preaching challenges are heightened when you have multiple ethnicities, cultures, and generations in your congregation. Each group has its own particularity, both in worship and in proclamation. If we are not aware of the differences, as a popular movie title suggests, things can be "lost in translation." In reality, the charge today is not just about preaching to multicultural congregations but preaching to the multiple identities that congregants inhabit, which include generation, class, ethnicity, political persuasion, and culture.

NIBS STROUPE: Our members expect that the sermon will touch their lives where they live and will encourage them in their struggles to know the reality of God's being at the center of their lives, as individuals and as part of American culture. Our members also expect that the sermon will address the theological view that God is the center of our lives and will be woven into the political realities that we all experience. By "political" I do not mean getting people elected to office but rather the distribution of power in our society. Almost half of our congregants will be subject to racial profiling as "minorities" when they walk out of the doors of our sanctuary, and all of our members swim in the sea of racism, sexism, materialism, militarism, homophobia, and many other cultural powers. While many of our members want sermons that are thought-provoking, many of our members also want and need sermons that are life-giving.

Those who come to us as members, whatever their racial or class category, come to us with an individualistic view of God and the church, where the emphasis is to enable people to get to heaven when they die. We seek to help them shift that view so that God's movement in our lives is not so much to help us find life after death but to find life in this life, especially when so much of our lives, in the American context, are lived in the midst of power of death. We seek to do this by emphasizing how political a document the Bible is, rooted in the liberation stories of the Exodus, schooled in the powerful prophetic tradition, and grounded in the life, death, and resurrection of Jesus Christ—a person who so radically challenged the political structures that he was executed as a revolutionary by the Roman Empire.

3) What (other) challenges does the diverse makeup of your congregation pose for you as a preacher? How have you addressed them? What strategies/ approaches have worked well? Which ones have not worked well?

JIN S. KIM: We have found it helpful to understand our congregational dynamics through family systems theory. We don't often realize how our families of origin and cultural practices shape our notions of "truth." In order to begin to understand each other, we have learned to ask critical and reflective questions both personally and corporately.

For how many generations have the main cultures that have influenced us in our childhood been a part of an imperial economic system? Were our great-grandparents the indigenous inhabitants of the land they lived on? Did the concept of landownership exist for our great-grandparents in the country where they lived as children? Did they have an ancestral connection to the land? Did they benefit from colonial conquest? Or were they harmed by it? Did our parents learn morality based on abstract principles or on a community-based ethic? What did our great-grandparents believe about the role of children in the family and in society? Were our parents taught to navigate complex social relationships, or were they raised to relate primarily to their nuclear family?

Through many years of counseling ministry it has become clear to me that white American culture is fundamentally neurotic. Certainly there is no society or culture devoid of members with mental health issues. However, there is something especially manipulative and emotionally violent about American culture, I suspect due more to denial about our genocide, ecocide, and slavery/Jim Crow than the history of violence itself. This uber-capitalist society has reduced human beings to a means of production. What does it mean to be "a productive member of society" when foreign workers, machines, and software regularly produce more and better than we do? I see a direct correlation between our society's growing inhumanity and the people's slide into mass mental deterioration.

Many of our members suffer from real feelings of depression and abandonment that keep them from being able to trust and participate in the rhythm of our community life. I have to say that the level of depression, anxiety, relational dysfunction, and emotional fragility among our white members has come as a surprise to many of our immigrant members who were fed the assumption of white supremacy our whole lives. Understanding the various sources of this emotional impoverishment has been a singular challenge. However, I am coming to understand how much suffering all our members live with on a daily basis, and hopefully I am also growing in compassion. I have also had to disclose my limitations frankly, and together we are learning to be church. Our people have shown extraordinary patience with me through this steep learning curve.

JACQUI LEWIS: When Trayvon Martin was shot and killed, our congregation put on hoodies and came to church. They did that because they were invited to in an e-mail that was part of an ongoing conversation about race in

America. One of our members wrote a song for Trayvon. We prayed, and we sang. We took up our arms to be more than multiracial, to be antiracist too. We decided as a community to talk more about race, more than we already did during our "justice arc," which is Martin Luther King Day through the end of Women's History Month. We started a class called "Erasing Race."

I am a black woman speaking to a multiracial community about race. Often. Almost always. Ferguson happened, and we dove deep into Black Lives Matter. Sometimes people tire of the justice emphasis, especially when their lives are feeling messy. "How can I be messy myself and heal the world?" they wonder. We work really hard to balance our calls to the particular demands of justice with a declaration that all lives are precious. Because we know that we are called by God to be bold about our faith, I preach the bold truth that God is on the side of those who are on the side of the marginalized. Our worship has included "die-ins" in which people lie down and interrupt the complacency of the ordinary. In the Black Lives Matter movement a die-in is often accompanied by a reading of the names of those killed by police violence. One of my sermons ended in a die-in. Baltimore happened. We preached about it. Gay Marriage, Trans Rights, Freedom to Choose, Women Must Speak and Lead, God Is Interreligious and We Should Be Too, and Black Lives Matter—these are all part of what it means when we say God is love.

Sometimes I preach fierce sermons. One recently started with "What in the hell is going on?" Sometimes I use humor to get us on board. One sermon recently began with: "Mom always said you will find what you are looking for. I thought she meant if I lost my pink sock in the dryer, I would find it. . . . I guess when that police officer in Baltimore looked at Freddie, he found a criminal. . . ." I will tell bad stories about myself, make myself vulnerable, invite vulnerability. Truth. Tears. Laughter. "Preaching is truth through personality," one sermon began, "and today I am feeling two things, total despair and hope . . . you give me hope . . ." I am a black clergywoman married to a white clergyman, and our stories show up in sermons as real examples of working for racial reconciliation every day. This works.

What does not work is being inauthentic. It does not work to pretend that we are the same because we are not. What works is to be as particular and rich with story and detail as I can. The particular has universal implications. What works is to be multivocal: illustrations that offer many portals in, rigorous exegesis always looking for the unusual take. They live for that. And in every sermon, I outline two or three actions congregation members can take because of what this text claims on our lives. You can march or you can tweet or you can sign this petition.

GABRIEL SALGUERO: Preaching in diverse congregations requires cultural sensitivity and intelligence so that God's word is delivered incarnationally. Incarnational preaching requires that we prepare for preaching and sermon delivery in such a way that the congregation knows we understand not only the scriptural texts we read but also where they're coming from. All good preaching is incarnational, giving attention to culture, race, class, and generational differences and similarities.

As a preacher I must not only navigate the diversity within Scripture itself but also be a pedestrian sociologist or cultural anthropologist. As a multi-frequency preacher I ask the question of Marvin Gaye, "What's going on?" and I do this across contexts. But I must also ask, "What does the gospel have to say to what's going on?" My task is to draw deeply from our sacred text and also the wells that shape and inform the diverse members of my congregation.

The truth is that the greatest challenge for my preaching has been navigating educational differences. I love using literature like Dostoyevsky, Cervantes, or Hugo. I feel more at home preaching for college-educated audiences. I once preached a sermon about the Kingdom of God as a critique of dystopian visions of the world. I began by comparing Isaiah's vision of the peaceable realm in Isaiah 11 with Aldous Huxley's *Brave New World* and George Orwell's *1984*. I loved what I had prepared because that is my preferred way of communicating. About a quarter of the way into the sermon I saw several parishioners with a glazed look in their eyes while I saw others furiously taking notes on their iPads. After the sermon I received both affirmation and critique. One parishioner said, "I can't wait to share this with my friends." Another parishioner said, "Pastor, ¡no sé de lo que hablastes! ("I have no idea what you're talking about!") What I had failed to do was communicate a vision of the Reign of God across vast educational differences.

NIBS STROUPE: Because we are mostly black and white in our congregational composition, we do not have the language issues in worship that many other multicultural churches have. Though we occasionally use Spanish and Korean and Japanese in our worship services, we are almost exclusively English-based. We seek to address the great differences in our congregation by concentrating on the biblical text in our sermons. We rarely use the lectionary in our sermons, but we choose themes and books of the Bible and work through them. We approach the Scriptures as narrative theology, using some examples and stories to accompany the text, of course, but mostly we count on the narrative of the text to be the vehicle for assisting the congregation to engage the living God in our midst today.

For example, we used the Letter to the Ephesians last fall as the text for our sermons. In this process, we took such phrases as "the prince of the power of the air" (Eph. 2:2, RSV) and sought to connect it not to the idea of a personalized devil but rather to our breathing in the air of life, while at the same time breathing in the pollutants of racism, militarism, and many other powers. In this sense we were "dead through the trespasses and sins" (2:1) but were given life through the grace of God through Jesus Christ. And this life that we were given is not just a connection to life after death but the powerful breakthrough of seeing ourselves no longer as "strangers and aliens" (2:19), alienated from one another by the dividing walls of the world, but rather as "citizens . . . and also members of the household of God" (2:19). In a multicultural congregation where these dividing walls must be taken seriously in order to survive, such a sermon becomes radical indeed.

Sometimes we change this approach, as in Black History Month and Women's History Month and Hispanic Heritage Month. In these seasons we seek to count on the experience of these diverse groups to work alongside the text as instructors for engaging God in our lives. We seek to address the internalized definitions of both white and male superiority and the idea of the inferiority of others.

4) How has your preaching changed as a result of ministering in/with your particular congregation? How do you balance being true to yourself and your own passions/interests/theology/style as a preacher while also being a faithful contextual preacher?

JIN S. KIM: My preaching has seven essential elements:

1. absolute conviction about what is being preached;
2. all theology and interpretation as provisionally true, at best;
3. all preaching is testimony and all testimony is preaching, when done right;
4. one must read well and integrally the Word, the world, the people, and where the Spirit is blowing;
5. the sermon is God's word to us today and must be preached with contextual urgency;
6. the preacher stands emotionally naked, so might as well go with it and be honest;
7. effective preaching means that the preacher must be willing to preach him or herself out of a job.

JACQUI LEWIS: I have been at Middle Church for twelve years. At first I thought my preaching was to help people feel safe and secure so that they would grow in faith and hang in with each other in this space of diversity. I thought preaching was to create a container that held them so that they could learn to play well together. I have come to know that preaching in this context is not about making people feel safe. We need only a good-enough environment in which to practice the ethics of the beloved community.

Preaching is about making people feel called to partner with God in the healing of themselves and the world. It is risky work, and we are called to do it. I am called to preach vision and help folk to see themselves in the vision. I am called to use the ancient sacred texts to help create a new text, a text we are writing with each other and with our God. I am called to help people grow in faith with my preaching and to find their own theological and ethical voices. I am called to help them to get real and go deep and let go of anything about God that impinges on their Holy creativity. I ask always: Am I attracting friends, retaining members, nurturing spirits, deploying activists, developing partners, and growing leaders?

If I am not true to myself while preaching, I am not preaching. My team of four clergy and I pray about a theme every year that we use the lectionary to develop: "God's Economy," "Deepening Spirit," "Creating a Just Society." We have an hour-long theology lab every week where we talk about the texts and themes and bring to the table what we are hearing in the congregation. We are exegeting the texts of Scripture, our culture, and our community when we preach.

GABRIEL SALGUERO: My preaching has changed in many ways as I seek to become a more hybrid and globally conscious preacher. I intentionally read more broadly and beyond North American sources. In addition, I intentionally attempt different styles of sermon delivery and structure. I do not feel it is inauthentic to try and faithfully engage the breadth of cultures and generations I seek to reach. In many ways it is a kenotic exercise that seeks to be faithful both to my own style and preferences and also to the people who listen to me.

Consider the sources many preachers use in their sermons. How many times do they quote from my favorite sources such as C. S. Lewis, Barbara Brown Taylor, Tom Long, Charles Spurgeon, or James Forbes? All are good sources, but there is a lack of diversity on so many levels. What about quoting more women, Asians, Hispanics, or African Americans? My preaching has been enriched by the wealth of global thinkers. I often ask new preachers to look over one year's worth of sermons and underline the people they quote. They are often fascinated to see the lack of representation of global voices in their own sermon preparation.

My cousin's wife, Jennifer, shared a funny story with me about a recent conversation with her son that points to this very question about communicating across generational diversity. Jennifer was frustrated with her son because he kept complaining over and over about the same thing. Finally she said to him, "Stop, already, you sound like a broken record." Her son replied, "Mommy, what's a record?" A lot of our preaching uses the language of record or CD with an iPod or smartphone generation. It's not that this generation is uninterested in what we have to say; it's that they have different cultural and linguistic currency. When we don't enter into people's worlds, they can't and most often won't hear us.

NIBS STROUPE: Between our Anglo and African American members, there is definitely a difference in the experience of the sermon, with our African American members expecting and living in a pattern of call and response. Over the years, I have shifted my approach from being manuscript oriented to being more holistic, where the manuscript, the text, and my own personality combine to produce a sermon that engages the whole person in the pew, including the mind and feelings. It has been a difficult shift for a Presbyterian Anglo trained in a mainline Presbyterian seminary forty years ago, but I find I am now much more personally engaged in preaching than I had been trained to be. That reality, of course, carries liabilities of its own, but I have found that I prefer this holistic approach. I still find myself frightened of my own narrative power, and that in itself serves as a balance for me.

I was raised in a white, Southern Presbyterian congregation that taught me about the love and grace of God and, at the same time, also taught me white supremacy, male domination, the centrality of money, and homophobia. My time as preacher at Oakhurst (thirty-two years) has forced me to see a different point of view so that I can challenge those weavings of matters of faith with politics, which a close friend of mine calls "the slave-holder captivity of the Bible." I can consider a different view without betraying my past or my faith. I can consider the biblical view that God has indeed broken down the barriers of the world and now invites us all, whatever our racial or class or gender category, to experience the liberating and life-changing grace of the God we know in Jesus Christ. Though I am no Saul on the road to Damascus, I do understand the power of conversion in a way that I would not have even imagined before becoming the pastor and preacher at multicultural Oakhurst Presbyterian Church. I am grateful for those who are different from me at Oakhurst and who have taken the risk to engage me at deep levels so that I might see where I was captured by the prince of the power of the air and, in so "seeing," could begin to take steps toward seeing myself and others as citizens and members of the household of God.

5) How do you preach in such a way that you respect differences (and encourage that respect within your congregation) while also helping unite the Body of Christ?

JIN S. KIM: What really gets through in a sermon is the preacher's disposition, for better and for worse. We have cultivated an intimate family dynamic at our church, so I can't hide my disposition, even if I tried. Whether the sermon has a pastoral bent or a prophetic edge, the congregation knows whether my heart is full of love or disdain. Maybe one can hide that in a manuscript but not in the oral art of preaching. This is one of the reasons I do not use any notes but use the Scripture text itself as my guide. I have also preached from the lectionary the entirety of my twenty-two years in full-time pastoral ministry—an important discipline for someone who has a strong opinion about everything.

My sermon preparation typically begins on Tuesday morning, when my staff are invited to give feedback on the previous Sunday's sermon. By Wednesday I have chosen a text and on Thursday some of us will have a lectionary discussion to advance understanding of the text but also to try out ideas. The most important task is to discern the spirit of the congregation. This must be a word to them, and not to any other flock. A couple of hours of commentary work on Saturday and final prep Sunday morning is my weekly routine.

JACQUI LEWIS: I have been inspired by the writings of Diogenes Allen on love, romance, and friendship to value the otherness of the other—to treat each person's particularity as a gift to be cherished. Love. Period. This is our deepest value. I have a diverse group of clergy who model the fact that we care about diversity. I pull from diverse resources—poetry, music, news sources—to speak to the multivocal nature of our community. I rarely think that I am uniting the Body of Christ. We are united by our hugs at the passing of the peace, by our choice to be there, by our common vision and mission. We are united by the ways we turn our love-power one week toward Black Lives Matter and another toward securing a real living wage for the people in our city and in our nation. We are united by our celebration of our differences. Celebrating our difference unites us. Using the particular stories of a particular person who represents a particular group of people makes us say, "Oh, I am like that. I have experienced that. I respect that." I find that being deeply particular carries with it universal appeal.

GABRIEL SALGUERO: Respecting differences does not mean that there cannot be unity. There is something about our shared humanity and God's love for all that can and should be highlighted even from our particularities. I have discovered that highlighting particularity and difference does not necessarily lead to balkanization and division. Multifrequency preaching can cause both a dissonance and consonance that deepens and broadens our understanding of God, the gospel, and each other. I remember one Sunday afternoon after using a classic Puerto Rican anecdote about a sister, a brother, a grandmother, and a dead chicken to illustrate grace that a Nigerian member said, "I never saw it that way, but it made grace clearer to me."

What I'm concerned about in my preaching is the idolizing of any form or method that continues to lead to segregated congregations. When we have monocultural or monoclass preaching that does not reflect the life of God in the communities we serve, we contribute to a segregated ecclesiology. I'm concerned that we seek to replicate Tom Long, Barbara Brown Taylor, Gardner Taylor, James Forbes, or any other model, just because these work in homogenous contexts. Of particular concern for me is the exporting of certain dominant preaching models from the United States as the normative models for preaching in global cities in late modernity. Preaching can have healthy models, but when all we have is one-size-fits-all, the church is the poorer for it. Preaching must reflect the life of God, and it is like a river that flows—like jazz.

NIBS STROUPE: I have come to have much more respect for the letters of Paul in the New Testament since I have been at Oakhurst Presbyterian. I much admire his words in 2 Corinthians 5:16. Where once I regarded him as a repressive and oppressive male dominator, my experience as pastor and preacher at Oakhurst has helped me gain deep appreciation for his attempt to bring multicultural groups together under the umbrella of the gospel of Jesus Christ. While I do not always agree with his decisions (or those of the people who wrote in his name), I do now understand so much better the complexity and difficulty of bringing diverse groups together under the proclamation of Jesus Christ as crucified Lord and Savior. I understand that none of us in our society have much practice at being sisters and brothers together. While those who are not Anglo have deep experience in learning how to live and survive in our Anglo world, none of us have significant experience at being peers together in the intimate setting of the community of faith, where we allow our deepest longings and fears and hopes and vulnerabilities to be expressed.

I seek to address this situation by emphasizing both our captivity to the categories of the world and the possibility of some liberation from those categories in the gospel of Jesus Christ. In doing this, I am not advocating that we diminish our differences into one melting pot of solidarity. Rather, I am advocating that we celebrate our diversity and use it as a stepping-stone in an affirmation of the unity we have in the Body of Christ. For instance, the text in Matthew 15:21–28 can become an important vehicle in this journey. The Gentile woman seems to genuinely convert Jesus on the value of Gentiles, and we are challenged by seeing Jesus as a human being, just like us. The idea of considering Jesus as a real person rather than God in human clothing is severely threatening to us, so much so that when I suggested this in a sermon at a presbytery meeting, I was charged with heresy by one Presbyterian church. Yet by the end of Matthew's Gospel, when the risen Jesus is sending out the disciples, he declines to send them only to the "lost sheep of the house of Israel" (Matt. 15:24). Rather, he tells them to "make disciples of all nations" (28:19). I'd like to think that his engagement with the Gentile woman in a multicultural context changed him and motivated him to see himself and his mission in a deeper and wider way—still Jewish, of course, but now inviting everyone in.

6) If you were to offer one piece of wisdom to preachers who are contemplating or just beginning their ministries in multicultural settings, what would it be?

JIN S. KIM: Multicultural ministry will complicate your life, your theology, your values, your politics, and your preaching, without question. My life was a lot simpler before when I was serving in a monocultural church context. I understand Korean people, and I know how Korean American churches function. But in my current church, there is no formula. The pastoral care needs of our members vary widely, and there isn't even a cultural normativity for the way we understand marriage or how to raise children. In many cases our grandparents were at war with one another. I've needed to challenge some of the values I've held most dear in order to lead this church with faith and courage. But I know I'm a better person and pastor through it all. My own family finds Church of All Nations to be a source of joy, nurture, and imagination. It has become our truest family.

JACQUI LEWIS: Become a student of culture. Read novels written by black women, Asian women, and Latino men. Listen to music that stretches you. Get commentaries by womanists and mujeristas and liberation theologians. Go hear some jazz and listen to Motown. Steep yourself in the richness of the varied cultures of our nation and become multicultural. Develop your border personality. Complexify issues. Get in the groove of both/and. Embrace ambiguity. Preachers need to live on the border and build bridges on the border. Jesus was a border person, a cultural mulatto. We who would preach in multiracial contexts would do well to be the same.

GABRIEL SALGUERO: My advice to preachers beginning their ministries in multicultural settings is to remember that preaching in highly diverse contexts is like jazz. Becoming a great jazz musician or composer is not just about improvisation; one must also know the basic scales extremely well. Only when we know the basics do we have the ingenuity and expertise to improvise. Knowing the Scriptures well is essential to engaging a myriad of hermeneutical approaches. The caution is always against engaging only one hermeneutical lens in our reading of Scripture. Jazz takes risks. Jazz as preaching requires drinking deeply from the well of Scripture, which in and of itself represents a great diversity of voices and perspectives. In addition, the jazz preacher must drink deeply from a variety of sources. She or he must read broadly across culture, class, and political ideology. This means that the sources we cite, the anecdotes we use, and the references to popular culture must come from a diversity of places.

One example I often use for jazz preaching is Jesus in John's Gospel. Jesus was a master communicator. Just consider his approaches in two adjacent chapters in John. In John 3 he is speaking at night to Nicodemus: a man, a Pharisee, and a person of influence. In John 4, he's speaking in the middle of the day to an unnamed Samaritan woman of a gender and a culture that were often marginalized. His approach to each of them was different because he took both Nicodemus and the Samaritan woman's lived reality seriously. No easy task, but certainly deeply enriching and transforming for the preacher and the listener.

If indeed Christians have a global ecclesiology, we should also have a global homiletics. Preaching for the global context starts with the conviction that the church has no national or ethnic monopoly. We are the church of Jesus Christ all over the world. As such, our preaching should celebrate that great diversity and gift. Moreover, preaching must engage the vernacular of those it seeks to reach. That can be Spanish, Mandarin, English, Twitter, American Sign Language, call and response, visual media, or sitting in silence. I think St. Paul's project in Romans 1 speaks directly to the hybrid and jazz preaching that has always been needed to engage the world. Paul's thesis is that the gospel is for the Jew and Greek, wise and unwise, learned and unlearned. To look at the preaching task as an extension of God's love for humanity is to remove it from parochialism toward hybridity. It is only when we see God working in every culture and generation that we can preach the whole gospel to the whole world.

NIBS STROUPE: Since I am a Presbyterian preacher, I'll divide my one piece of wisdom into three parts. First, approach the Bible as the multicultural document that it is. It is set in the midst of a group of people determined to be exclusive but whose God keeps widening the boundaries. Second, in the American context, keep race on the table. It is one of the central driving forces in American cultural history, and it has permeated us all, just as has the prince of the power of the air. We have lived as a multicultural congregation for over fifty years, and we have survived primarily through God's leading us to continue to do battle with this principality and power. Finally, help yourself and your congregation to live in the reality that God has broken down the dividing walls of hostility in Jesus Christ. In looking through that break, what we find are not the monsters whom we have been taught to fear but rather the brothers and sisters for whom our hearts are longing.

Chapter 7

Mixing It Up in Athens, or
How to Proclaim Good News to Young
Adults Who Are Waiting for the Next Thing

ANNA CARTER FLORENCE

How do we proclaim good news to young adults who are on the margins of church or have left it?

While Paul was waiting for them in Athens, he was deeply distressed to see that the city was full of idols. So he argued in the synagogue with the Jews and the devout persons, and also in the marketplace every day with those who happened to be there. Also some Epicurean and Stoic philosophers debated with him. Some said, "What does this babbler want to say?" Others said, "He seems to be a proclaimer of foreign divinities." (This was because he was telling the good news about Jesus and the resurrection.) So they took him and brought him to the Areopagus and asked him, "May we know what this new teaching is that you are presenting? It sounds rather strange to us, so we would like to know what it means." Now all the Athenians and the foreigners living there would spend their time in nothing but telling or hearing something new.

Then Paul stood in front of the Areopagus and said, "Athenians, I see how extremely religious you are in every way. For as I went through the city and looked carefully at the objects of your worship, I found among them an altar with the inscription, 'To an unknown god.' What therefore you worship as unknown, this I proclaim to you. The God who made the world and everything in it, he who is Lord of heaven and earth, does not live in shrines made by human hands, nor is he served by human hands, as though he needed anything, since he himself gives to all mortals life and breath and all things. From one ancestor he made all nations to inhabit the whole earth, and he allotted the times of their existence and the boundaries of the places where they would live, so that they would search for God and perhaps grope for him and find him—though indeed he is not far from each one of us. For 'In him we live and move and have our being'; as even some of your own poets have said, 'For we too are his offspring.' Since we are

God's offspring, we ought not to think that the deity is like gold, or silver, or stone, an image formed by the art and imagination of mortals. While God has overlooked the times of human ignorance, now he commands all people everywhere to repent, because he has fixed a day on which he will have the world judged in righteousness by a man whom he has appointed, and of this he has given assurance to all by raising him from the dead." When they heard of the resurrection of the dead, some scoffed; but others said, "We will hear you again about this." At that point Paul left them. But some of them joined him and became believers, including Dionysius the Areopagite and a woman named Damaris, and others with them. (Acts 17:16–34)

*T*hey called him a babbler. It wasn't a compliment, either: spermalogos, which isn't quite what it sounds like in English, but almost. Seed picker. Word scrapper. Someone who spouts childish, raggedy nonsense, and, worse, profits from it. A gossip columnist, say, or the blogger who posts nothing but recycled chatter. The person you delete from your Twitter account when you've had enough foolishness. "What does this babbler want to say?!" the Athenians muttered about Paul, and Paul must have known he was in trouble. This audience was not going to be like the others he'd encountered on his missionary journeys. This one was going to take some thought. How do you proclaim good news in a city filled with students, a city obsessed with all things new? How do you preach in Athens?

Changing Tactics

Before his arrival in Athens, Paul's track record as a preacher wasn't bad. At least he'd always made an impression, if you count thrilling the faithful, disturbing the authorities, and getting arrested, beaten, and thrown out of town "an impression." Simply put, Paul was a preacher who turned heads, and his preaching usually led to (1) the founding of a small band of believers and (2) the disgruntlement of everyone else. His general practice, when entering a new city, was to make his way to the synagogue, set up camp, and immediately begin to argue about the Scriptures with anyone who happened to be there. He argued in Corinth, he argued in Ephesus. And he was good at it—really good. Paul was a lawyer; he could argue for three weeks without stopping, if necessary, and sometimes did. It was a homiletical tactic that worked for him, or at least came naturally. And if sometimes the citizens of a place tired of it, as happened in Thessalonica, around the time our story begins; if they decided that his arguments were offensive and his presence no longer welcome—well, Paul was used to that, too. He knew how to leave town in a hurry, if he had to. He knew how to shake the dust from his feet and move on to the next place.

Originally, that was all Athens was supposed to be: the next place. Paul's visit to Thessalonica and environs had ended rather abruptly when a group of angry citizens began hunting for him throughout the countryside; obviously, it was time to *go*, and fast. Escorts led Paul to the coast and took him as far as Athens, where angry Thessalonians might not think to look and where a preacher could presumably blend into the lively atmosphere of teachers and philosophers. In Athens Paul could wait for Timothy and Silas, his companions, to catch up with him. In Athens he could get his bearings and figure out what was next.

But Athens was different. Athens struck Paul in a way no city ever had before. It was all the idols; he walked around, the text says, and his spirit was deeply disturbed to see that the Athenians had so many of them. There were idols, or statues, to the gods of beauty and youth, the gods of wisdom and intellect, the gods of wine and war, the gods of light and hearth and sea and fire. Every human need and craving and desire and skill was manifest in a physical representation that Paul could see only as idolatrous. It provoked him to his core. It sent him stomping to the synagogue and the marketplace to argue with the Athenians about it. And as anyone but Paul might have predicted, his arguments fell flat. You cannot preach to people you have just met when you are already furious with them. You cannot offer good news *and* a scathing lifestyle critique at the same time, particularly if you have just arrived in a place. It makes your sermon sound like ranting and raving, or, as the Athenians helpfully suggested, like babbling nonsense. And babblers are easily dismissed.

Athens was different. It was ancient and hip and artsy and fascinated by what's next, and it was the first city to offer Paul a real homiletical challenge. Even he could see that if he didn't change tactics, he was going to miss the narrow window of attention the Athenians always offered the new person or idea in town. Arguing wouldn't do it in Athens; the Athenians practically *invented* arguing. It wasn't anything new to them, and they would want to hear something new. So what to do with his sliver of time, when it came?

Wait for It

The first thing Paul did was to stop talking. He literally shut up, which is a useful thing for a preacher to do, from time to time: be quiet and take stock of your surroundings. Do not assume that just because you know how to preach, everyone wants to hear you do it. Wait for an invitation. Know that this invitation might or might not be to a conventional pulpit: there are many forums for speech, and these vary from context to context. Perhaps you will be invited into a space that looks familiarly sacred with a pulpit you can easily identify. On the other hand, perhaps you won't, and if you cannot be watchful and creative about the space you are dealt, you are going to miss out. First, however, and most important, is the invitation. Do not speak until you are invited.

Paul had to think hard about this. It was not in his nature to hold back or to refrain from offering vocal opinions and explanations in any and all circumstances. Paul was charismatic to his very pores: he *loved* proclamation. But in Athens, he learned to wait, which was not a verb to which he gravitated but one God kept sending him, all the same. Wait, Paul. Wait for Silas and Timothy. Wait for the Athenians. Let them extend the invitation to speak to them in their own time and on their own turf.

When the invitation finally came, it was not for Paul to deliver the message at a local Greek temple on interfaith night. Instead, he was asked to appear at the Areopagus, the rocky hillside that had once functioned as an Athenian high court of law and where even the god Ares was said to have been tried. The Areopagus was not a temple but a popular spot for Athenians to hear and debate one another. It was also where they gathered to tell and hear something new: in this case, to hear Paul talk about his strangely fascinating foreign divinities. Paul was astute enough to realize that this was his moment and he had better seize it. He could be offended by the fact that he was the latest curiosity, or he could take his fifteen minutes of fame when it was offered. He could hold out for an idol-free environment, or he could set aside his own aversions and figure out how to preach in the presence of statues that made his skin crawl. The invitation, when it comes, is often a thing that requires patience and adaptation as well as a healthy dose of restraint.

Look for It

The second thing Paul did was to take a closer look at the Athenians themselves. First impressions are instructive but not always accurate; perhaps there is more to see than you originally thought. Perhaps your initial assessment of the Athenians as a godless, rudderless set of trend-sucking, ego-driven techno-junkies was a bit premature. Look again. Look slowly. Walk the streets and take your time. Stop at the coffee shop and start a conversation with the barista and the person sitting at the corner table. Ask about what they're working on and what they're thinking about. Ask for their recommendations about what you should see and do while you're in the neighborhood. Follow through on their suggestions. Expect to be surprised. Suspend judgment about this. Let wonder and delight speak; hold shock in check.

Keep looking. When you begin to appreciate what you see, you will know you are paying attention at last. Take a deep breath and look again.

Paul was a keen observer, but an opinionated one. He had a hard time suspending judgment about what he saw (*Athens = idols; Athenians = idolatrous*), especially if it triggered in him some deeply held belief. In Athens, he was confronted by the most blatant violation of the second commandment that he had ever encountered: the sight of *so many* idols, so many graven images. It was practically blinding. He could hardly think straight, let alone see straight. And zooming in for a closer look? Who would want to?

Memory, however, is another sort of trigger, and every bit as powerful. One verb recalls another or sets in motion an experience that flickers just below the surface, and even the most opinionated moment is up for revision. Paul knew about mistaken first impressions. He knew about belief so ferocious that it required an intervention of blindness. His new life with Jesus started on the Damascus Road. And maybe it was this that gave him a special sensitivity to knee-jerk reactions, whenever they appeared. Maybe it was this that allowed him to push past his inclination to smash those idols and instead to take another look at them.

What he saw was a kind of empty canvas: the statue to the *unknown* god, jammed in between the grander statues to the gods of love and sex and power and so forth. It was a small ache, a small openness to what might yet be out there, as if the Athenians were saying, *Even this glory cannot speak to every human need. Even we are still searching for something not yet revealed.* If Paul hadn't been paying close attention, he would have sailed right past it; if he hadn't been examining the idols with interest, he would have missed its significance. He would have gotten all caught up in the flashiness of machinery and technology, which are not, in the end, what display our humanity. If you want to know the pulse of a place, look at how it marks its own borders. Look for what it is yearning and searching for beyond those borders. Find its idols, and then find the one that is missing.

The text may be having a quiet laugh with us in this part of the story. Don't just take a second look; take a second look at the very things that make you want to look *away*. Take a second look at the idols: the ones that repulse you most, the ones you love to hate, the ones that go against everything you stand for. Examine them closely, because in them you will find the opening. In them you will find the entry point to dialogue and conversation about our common human ache. And just so you know: those idols, the ones you scrutinize so carefully, will actually put your own into sharp relief. Another culture's statue to the unknown god will probably show you that you had one, too, all along.

Speak to It

The third thing Paul did was to put all this into words. It is one thing to have a stunning insight; it is quite another to summon the courage to say it out loud, in words that others will understand. Paul did both in this sermon. It is one of the few complete spoken texts of his that we have, and it is powerful to read. We can only imagine what it must have been like to hear.

Several things stand out. One is Paul's starting point: he begins not with himself but with what he has seen—and not in Jerusalem or Damascus, either, but what he has seen in Athens, as a guest. He begins with a witness about the Athenians themselves. He describes a moment, while walking their streets and marketplaces and temples and meeting grounds, when he saw something intriguing: the statue to the unknown god. It lets the Athenians know that he has taken the time to really see them. It lets them know he has come with interest and appreciation rather than criticism. And it lets them know that he is a careful observer and therefore someone to be trusted. A good witness is a good conversation partner. Paul establishes himself as a witness first, a witness in Athens.

He also establishes himself as a student of their culture. He knows their literature; he quotes their poets. He can do it without stumbling over the words, which tells us that he has not only read the work but absorbed it, understood it, and even appreciated it. He sticks with material that is appropriate to illustrate his point rather than material that crosses the line into *extremely awkward* territory. And most important: he seems to know that nothing is worse than preachers who try to pass for cooler or younger or more Athenian than they actually are. Nothing is worse than preachers who pretend that they are residents of a culture to which they are rightfully only witnesses. Paul gets it: you have to be authentic. You can observe, but you don't get to live there. So observe well; cite well. Don't be an embarrassment to yourself or the Athenians by trying to be someone you aren't.

There is a reason for all this observation and citation, however, and that is to find the moments of intersection between gospel and culture. Paul does this with the image of the unknown god. He does it carefully and respectfully. "I see you are very religious," he tells the Athenians. "I see it in your places of worship and I see it in this remarkable place holder: the statue to an unknown god. So now I want to tell you where you and I meet, and it is in this very image! What you worship as unknown, I now proclaim to you!"

This is the moment when Paul lets it rip, as it were. He doesn't hold back. He doesn't save anything for later. He tells the Athenians, as joyfully and simply as he can, that the god they have been searching for is the One who has come to us in Jesus Christ. He tells the story. He tells it as a witness who has seen and believed. And he lets God's verbs predominate: *God* is the One who has sent. *God* is the One who has raised from the dead. *God* is the One who has redeemed. It is all there, in plain sight, even in Athens. Paul makes it sound as if Christ himself is present and walking through the Areopagus with them—which, of course, Christ is.

Afterward

The Athenians listen. Some of them are intrigued. Some of them scoff. Some want to hear more, later. Paul knows: this is as it should be. The gospel is scandalous to the ear and eye, and if preachers got a standing ovation with every sermon, they might forget exactly how scandalous it really is. They might begin to think that they themselves are the subject of the sermon, which they are not. God is the subject. Even in Athens, God is the subject. And telling the story is more important than smashing idols.

How do we proclaim good news to young adults who are on the margins of church or have left it or are waiting for the next thing? How do we proclaim good news in Athens?

We make a beginning. We find the empty plinth and that small placeholder of a statue. We put away our aversions and our arguments and uncork some joy, which always bubbles up when we tell the story. And we have a good story to tell! So tell it. Tell it as a joyful witness. Go to Athens, get to know some Athenians, and take it from there.

Chapter 8

Prophesy to the Bones

RICHARD LISCHER

How do we preach to a church that is increasingly depressed and discouraged because of the loss of "church" as it once was?

*I*n his essay "Falling into Ministry, Learning about Death," Thomas G. Long takes the reader back to his South Carolina childhood for the funeral of his beloved Uncle Ed. He remembers with love and gratitude a small church's ministry to his family. When the minister arrives for the funeral in his "off-the-rack preacher suit," Long recalls, he brought with him "the sudden awareness that we were not merely there to bury a dead relative but to venture out on a sacred pilgrimage."[1] In this essay and in his earlier book, *Accompany Them with Singing: The Christian Funeral*, Long deftly establishes the genius of "church" and outlines the church's best practices in the face of death.

But what are we to say when it is the church itself that is dying?

How does one address a congregation's corporate sense of loss? It is a sober and realistic question that is rarely addressed in seminary classrooms or church growth conferences. Our notions of preaching include the comfort of the gospel in the face of loss, but the word "preach" itself, from the Greek *euaggelízo* or *kerússo*, which mean "to tell good news" or "to proclaim as a herald," is linguistically freighted with triumph and success. *Proclaim*—to a congregation about to go under? The very idea is a contradiction in terms. Speaking of failure seems all wrong in a culture congenitally oriented to success. Well-known preachers on the circuit are rarely invited into the pulpits of congregations struggling to survive. The visiting preacher may not have a word for churches in hospice care.

And this is as it should be. For such preaching is not work for outsiders. The congregation's losses may be discussed in study groups, informal gatherings, and in sorrowful—or sometimes acrimonious—church meetings at which matters of attendance, building maintenance, and finances are open

98

for prolonged discussion. The conversation may be triggered by declining attendance, financial strains, a schism within the membership, or the impending closure and sale of church property that some traditions call "deconsecration." But at bottom, the issue is theological. It may be approached by way of numbers and logistics, but numbers should not be given the last word. God gets the final word, and the preacher, as the publicly appointed steward of the Word, is called to address all losses among the faithful and "to sustain the weary with a word" (Isa. 50:4b).

As Ezekiel looks out on the vast cemetery that was once a vibrant and viable Israel, the Lord asks, "Mortal, can these bones live?" to which the prophet gives the perfect answer, "O Lord GOD, [only] you know" (Ezek. 37:3). Then God commands Ezekiel, "Prophesy to these bones" (v. 4). Speak to the gone ones. Speaking to, and not merely about, is the vocation of both the shepherd and the prophet.

All Our Losses

The sense of loss among Christian congregations is gaining relevance at a disheartening rate. From 1965 to 2012, not a single year passed in which eight mainline Protestant denominations did not decline. Not one magical, miraculous year. These losses have been "offset" by gains among Church of God, Assemblies of God, African Methodist Episcopal, and Southern Baptist congregations, though it is always a mistake to view the disappearance of worshippers from a community as "cancelled out" or "balanced" by statistical gains elsewhere. While some have argued that the rate of decline among Protestants is leveling off, the most recent Pew Research survey documents the accelerating slide among all age groups, races, and geographical regions. From 2007 to 2014 the number of people in the United States identifying themselves as Christian declined by a staggering 7.8 percent.[2]

The fadeout is occurring more rapidly among young adults—many of whom list their religious affiliation as "none"—whose drift away from church effectively places the mantle of leadership where it has always been, across the backs of the graying faithful. The statistics remain abstract until the pews begin to empty in your church, the fuss and laughter of children is no longer heard, and the congregation begins living off its endowment, if it has one. The situation becomes painfully concrete when the budget no longer supports the maintenance of the "church plant" or the vital works of ministry for which the church was widely recognized in the community.

Among Catholics in the United States, the decline is also occurring in absolute numbers, this despite the unprecedented influx of Hispanic Catholics into the church. Dwindling attendance in mostly challenged urban parishes, as well as the shortage of priests and other religious, has dictated the enforced closure or merger of thousands of once-viable parishes throughout the country. In some cases, bishops have shuttered thriving parishes in well-to-do areas in order to avoid the blatant injustice of penalizing only poor churches. Many Catholics, like the devout, middle-aged woman with whom I recently spoke, whose early life was formed in an urban Irish American parish in upstate New York, mourn the loss of the sacred ground in which their faith took root. One of the treasures of a lifetime has been stolen. The remnant is left with nothing more than memories of the years when St. Cecilia's or Holy Name was a badge of religious and ethnic pride and the single most important place in the neighborhood.

The drama of the church's storied memories was the subject of James Hopewell's 1987 book, *Congregation*, which traced the rich and generative veins of congregational identity.[3] By surveying cultures and mythic plots, Hopewell reminded us that a congregation not only lives in a culture (a la H. R. Niebuhr's *Christ and Culture*) but also is a culture replete with its own traditions and narratives. It has a corporate personality. Anyone who has ever watched an entire congregation grieve, clap its hands, or step out in faith understands that a congregation is something other than the sum of its parts.

Using the trope of the house to symbolize congregation, Hopewell identified three standard modes of "reading" the life of a congregation, to which he added a less-familiar fourth. The first hermeneutic tool in assessing a congregation he labeled *contextual*. It analyzes the church's life by observing its role and function in the life around it—the neighborhood and culture in which it is situated. If P. T. Forsyth defined theology as "the gospel taking the age seriously," the sociological approach examines the degree to which the congregation communicates with and serves its neighbors. How seriously does it address the assumptions and aspirations of its age?

The *mechanistic* approach views the church as an engine whose systems must perform well if the church is to survive. How are decisions made? What are its internal processes of communication? Does it have an effective method of reaching outsiders? Does the staff function as a team? How much money is required to keep the engine running? According to mechanistic theories, effective planning and the application of proper methods will produce the expected result—church growth. Breakdowns in these procedures will lead to stagnation and decline.

The third hermeneutic is *organic*. Many years ago, my wife and I were trying to sell our home without a real estate agent, which meant that we showed the house ourselves. I had a rehearsed spiel in which I testified (with accompanying hand gestures) to the physical advantages of the house: the new kitchen appliances, the automatic garage opener, the ample closet space. The first time I gave the speech, a potential buyer cut me off. "Tell me," she asked, "can you raise a family in this house?" She was asking the organic question. The organic approach is not impressed by the size and utility of the plant. It addresses the more qualitative aspects of the congregation, such as community, vitality, and participation. It is the loss of home or family that many grieve when a church fails.

Hopewell's fourth reading, and the one I find most helpful when addressing a corporate sense of loss, is *symbolic*. Ask a family about the state of its life, and chances are you will hear a story. It is often the story of the best or, more likely, the worst thing that ever happened to them. "How long have you lived in High Point?" "We came here twenty-five years ago because our parents wanted to get into the furniture business, but the whole industry went south, and we lost our money. Then Dad died. Here we are." Ask a church about its faltering ministry, and it will summon its communal memory and gather its accumulated symbols in order to tell you the story of its life—how the neighborhood changed and the majority of members fled to the suburbs, or how the bishop broke his promise to send an effective young leader to "grow" the church, or how "we just plain aged out" and lost our mojo for innovative ministry. In the passage cited above, Tom Long remembers his childhood church symbolically, as "a sacred pilgrimage."[4]

The pastoral response to loss will begin with the congregation's corporate story. The preacher who is sensitive to the symbolic dimensions of ministry will learn to bypass mechanical issues and focus instead on the church's narrative. According to Hopewell, that story will likely be a hybridized tale of romantic adventure (Long's "venture") followed in some cases by the tragic experience of betrayal or failure.[5] Preaching to the narrative creates a bond among the remaining members. This is our story. We inhabit it together. The preacher uses the congregation's given name, "Trinity" or "St. Paul's," as if addressing a single person. She names it for what it still is: one holy body.

Not every decline in numbers, however, represents failure or an unhappy ending. As a congregation and its pastor rehearse their story, they must discern the crucial difference between loss and change. Is the story over? Shall the congregation face facts and aim at "dying well"? Or is it still possible to discern amid altered circumstances the seeds of resurrection and the indistinct outline of a new ministry?

In the early 1950s, a suburban congregation in the Midwest named "Redeemer" was founded by migrating members of several urban churches.

In pace with the post-war population of its suburb, the young church grew at a phenomenal rate. At its peak in the late '50s it was holding four worship services and three Sunday school sessions weekly. Every week one thousand children attended Sunday classes. Hundreds were baptized and confirmed. The church's personality, if it had one, was that of a sprouting, gangly adolescent whose only apparent purpose in life was to grow. The homogeneity of its members was defined by their German ethnicity and denominational roots in the city and, even more significantly, by their shared exhilaration with suburban living. In those years, the church served as a guide in the migration and acculturation of its members.

More than fifty years later, the same suburb and the same congregation have reached capacity. The modest bungalows of the post-war subdivisions from which the church drew its strength now appear subpar at best. The original settlers have died, and their children have moved away to starter-castles in more distant suburbs or rehabilitated bungalows in a gentrifying urban core. The homogeneity of the 1950s and '60s has given way to shifting alliances of races and ethnic groups. Today, migration originates not from the dry bones of the inner city but from Mexico and Central America. Over the decades new and unfamiliar churches have taken the field and surrounded "Fort Redeemer." Statistically, the original church has declined, but in the years of its diminishment its mission has been repurposed. It has evolved from growth to ministry. Redeemer now fosters a new and more radical sense of community among its members. Its school is no longer an instrument of church growth but a genuine ministry of education for those in need. The congregation understands itself as a redemptive and reconciling presence in what has become a diverse and often-conflicted community. It is no longer the rock star of its denomination or the outsized and awkward adolescent in the community. Redeemer is smaller but far surer of its God-given identity and purpose.

A more dramatic narrative is recounted by journalist Robert King in an article on the "Death and Resurrection of an Urban Church." A United Methodist congregation founded in the late 1920s grew to its apogee, in the 1950s, of 2,300 members. Just as quickly, or so its story goes, the racial composition of the surrounding neighborhoods changed, and white flight reduced the once-proud congregation to weekly attendance of seventy-five. This was death. It was prelude, however, to a most unpredictable series of resurrections. The first resurrection was achieved by means of attention to social justice issues and community needs, such as food and clothing pantries and youth basketball programs. The pastor who helped achieve this breakthrough then departed. When he returned a decade later, the same pastor "read" his earlier success as an exercise in doing for people what they should be doing for others. Despite the many church programs, life in the neighborhood had deteriorated. He interpreted the earlier resurrection as a series of well-intentioned efforts that created receptacles rather than agents of ministry. This was the death of genuine discipleship. He therefore encouraged a second resurrection, one of discovered vocation, in which popular and well-intentioned programs were scrapped and the skills and capacities of the former recipients of ministry were utilized by the community. This continues to be a risky prophetic move, but it represents the true empowerment of the church. It can only be told as a story—not of loss but change.[6]

The Metanarrative Has Shifted

Aside from local stories of decline or change, many Christians are living in a more notional metanarrative of the loss of "church" as they once knew it. Our assumptions concerning the nature and role of church have gradually succumbed to other realities. Older Christians were formed by the consensus-model of church in which the Reformation-based denominations dominated the religious landscape. Culturally and theologically, most people understood the similarities and differences between a Lutheran and a Presbyterian or a Methodist and a Baptist—and the differences mattered. In 1960, the year Will Herberg published his best-selling *Protestant, Catholic, Jew*, the title alone captured the perceived religious situation in America. Invitations to the White House or the presidential inaugural rotated among the respected representatives of a few established traditions. In that era, urban churches began migrating in whole or in part to the suburbs, which were seen by many as the land of unlimited Protestant opportunity.

A decade or so later, a critique of the "suburban captivity of the church" reimagined church as a countercultural movement in step with dramatic social changes occurring nationwide. It was an exciting time to be Christian in America. From Selma, Alabama, Martin Luther King Jr. issued his ecumenical appeal to churches and synagogues across the land, and thousands came to march for freedom. In succeeding decades, however, the socially conscious churches, including African American congregations on the vanguard of the struggle for civil rights, found it difficult to sustain the radical edge of an era that was passing. Among white progressives, the liberalism that had once revolted against the "dead hand" of orthodoxy managed to survive, if only as a less interesting and equally moribund form of orthodoxy. Even the fiery evangelical and charismatic churches failed to escape the ecclesial version of gentrification. Many of the independent bodies have eased into the status of para-denominations with corporate-like administrative structures and a newfound social respectability. Their clergy now hold forth at presidential prayer breakfasts.

The pan-global growth of Christianity continues to present a stark contrast to the decline of North American churches. Christians in the United States recognize the movements of the Spirit around the world, but we are nonetheless shocked that there are more Christians in China than "Christian America" or that the average member of the worldwide Anglican Communion is not a commuter in Connecticut but a villager in Nigeria. Thus, for many, the changing religious paradigms are tinged with loss. Some Christians have embraced their new identity as minority-status witnesses, while others have forsaken both the comforts and disappointments of church altogether in favor of a highly individualized spirituality, recently defined by America's newest public theologian, *New York Times* columnist David Brooks, as "an inner sense of relationship to a higher power that is loving and guiding."[7]

I have sketched several dimensions of the church's sense of loss in the bleakest of terms for two reasons. First, the loss is real. Churches are struggling; some are closing. The numbers don't lie. More than one bishop has said to me, "Face up to it."

Second, in the United States the decline is so steep and pervasive that it eliminates the perennial tendency to "fix" the problem with new programs or ecclesial restructuring. The church responds to loss by relying on its Lord and by embracing the essential tasks that set it apart as church in the first place. To give a current example, the buoyancy of spirit recently observed among Catholics stems not from more sophisticated methods of communication but from a pope's willingness to put his theological understanding of the poor into practice and to translate it into a new idiom of leadership. As Jeremiah says of the great king Josiah, "He judged the cause of the poor and needy . . . Is not this to know me?" (Jer. 22:16).

What to Say

Not long ago I took part in an interdisciplinary panel on "What to Say When Someone Is Dying." The panel included a nurse, an oncologist, a cultural critic, and a theologian. Frankly, I didn't envision much interest in the topic, especially in a busy and successful university such as ours. The (to me) surprising interest generated by the discussion appeared to reflect the problem we all experience in the face of death: we have many methods of treating the approach of death, but when it happens we don't know what to say.

One cannot help but notice the similarities between ministry to a dying person and ministry to a dying church. The first rule for caregivers is to listen. By attending to the congregation's experience, the preacher will be given the word that is needed. Like a dying person, a congregation in hospice care has unfinished business—the loose ends of unreconciled factions, the symbolic work of closure, the fundamentally human need to be remembered. As with a dying person, the congregation experiences tremendous assurance in the presence of a caring human being. In this situation, the pastor is no longer a conduit for God's word but its incarnation. In Urban Holmes's evocative phrase, the priest becomes a "symbol bearer."

As with a dying person, a dying congregation does not require explanation but solidarity. There is no more helpful word than a friend's promise: "I will go with you." One of my favorite prayers begins, "O Lord, you know the deep places through which our lives must pass." The preacher's word reflects the Lord's acquaintance with deep places. The word is a promise, not a proof. It is the proffered word of someone you trust. As with a dying person, the death of a congregation is marked by the language of intimacy. There are words that only a pastor or trusted leader can invoke: thank, love, bless, release.

In our panel discussion, the oncologist began by making a great point. Even if you are dying, you are not dead yet! This means that the terminally ill person remains an agent of ministry with the capacity to shape the circumstances surrounding his or her death. He may do everything in his power to relieve the suffering and grief of those who care for him. She may forgive those who have hurt her or promote reconciliation among her estranged children. The dying person discovers that he or she possesses great authority. Because the witness to faith is given at the brink of death, it bears extraordinary power.

So also the remaining members of a dying congregation may reinforce their corporate identity as a holy body. They do so by avoiding recrimination and showing extraordinary kindness toward one another. They may rededicate themselves to the holy things all Christians can do: they can support and care for one another, visit the sick, and continue to study the word of God and celebrate the Eucharist. A declining congregation may eliminate many of its ministry programs with a view toward focusing on one area of expertise. The congregation may have cut staff, which in turn has caused it to cancel vacation Bible school, the bell choir, and expensive youth jamborees. It may choose, however, to focus much of its remaining energy on a particular activity it has always done well, perhaps its food or shelter ministry.

But what to say? The pastor tells her congregation its own story in such a way that it is braided with the narrative of God's faithfulness. The story will include elements of lament and celebration—of crucial losses and the triumph of many Easter mornings. The story is worth reprising several times over so long as it is incorporated into the larger story of God's providential care and redemption of the world.

The liturgies of the church can help turn lament to thanksgiving as members physically touch and bless the symbolic sites of God's goodness—the baptismal font at the front of a sanctuary, the wooden cross salvaged from "the old church" that burned in 1952, the window in a multiracial church portraying a dark and a light hand clasped in friendship, the kitchen and coffee urn in the church's basement, where good gossip regularly became gospel. These are the ways a church confesses: "You gave us these symbols and this history. We now return them to you, their rightful Owner." This church has completed its mission. Every story has an end. Our story has ended neither with a bang nor a whimper, but with a blessing: "Well done, good and faithful servant."

Three Languages of Loss

1. Exile

Three biblical modes of speech undergird the preacher's ministry to a congregation's corporate grief. They are rough templates for our preaching. The first mode addresses the experience of exile as interpreted by the prophets. The analogy to exile is only partial, however. Some of the prophets understood exile as a result of Israel's faithlessness. Jeremiah might well have pronounced God's judgment on the North American church for its idolatry of power, its subservience to the state, its support of war, and its easy accommodation to secular culture. The contemporary preacher might render such a judgment on American religion, and as a historical and theological generalization it would be true. But the influential churches most answerable for these sins appear to be growing stronger while the weak struggle to survive. It is not like God, or God's prophets, to single out the weakest members of society (or the *ecclesia*) for punishment.

Beyond judgment, the prophetic idiom is characterized by the prophet's intuition of loss. The emotion most characteristic of Israel's prophets is not

anger but sorrow. The prophets offer the assurance of God's continuing presence among those who have been lost or dislocated. Even Jeremiah, the most
uncompromising of Israel's critics, who counsels his people to accept and
even embrace exile—even Jeremiah performs a symbolic act of redemption
when he buys his cousin's field at Anathoth, thereby indicating that despite
the bleakest of prospects, the basic responsibilities of kinship will continue
(Jer. 32:6b–15). Further, in the face of long-term exile, Jeremiah conveys
a promise to Israel whose hopefulness resonates with future generations of
uprooted and disoriented people. The exiled congregation may not be restored
to its precise place of abundance. But the prophet envisions a new covenant
that does not depend on sacred space or external symbols. "I will put my law
within them, and I will write it on their hearts; and I will be their God, and
they shall be my people" (Jer. 31:33).

Perhaps because he himself went into exile, Ezekiel surpasses Jeremiah
in his empathic understanding of those who have been dislocated from their
familiar place of worship. The prophet sits in silent, stupefied solidarity with
those who have been removed from their homes. Like the best of pastors, he
reports, "I sat where they sat." When he surveys the devastation of Israel,
symbolized by a vast expanse of dry bones, he has no plan but to wait on the
Lord for further developments. Ezekiel is given the promise of resurrection
by means of the new and unpredictable breath of the Spirit. "I prophesied as
he commanded me, and the breath came into them, and they lived, and stood
on their feet, a vast multitude" (Ezek. 37:10). God's restoration of Israel shat-
ters the eerie silence of the cemetery and replaces it with the clatter of dry
bones coming together.

If Ezekiel's noisy experience breathes the spirit of hope, the tone of Second Isaiah is one of sheer joy. Accusations against Israel play a minor role in
Second Isaiah, but promises to the exiles, hopeful utterance, and oracles of
salvation are everywhere.[8]

> Comfort, O comfort my people,
>   says your God.
> Speak tenderly to Jerusalem,
>   and cry to her
> that she has served her term . . .
>   (Isa. 40:1–2a)

Once again we can see the analogy between speaking to an individual
and speaking to a corporate entity. What scholars believe were oracles originally intended for individuals Second Isaiah addresses to the company of
exiles:

> "I have chosen you and not cast you off";
> do not fear, for I am with you,
>   do not be afraid, for I am your God.
>   (Isa. 41:9b–10a)

In Second Isaiah God is Redeemer (e.g., Isa. 51:10). For dispirited Christians, like their forbears in exile, the notion of redemption reaches back to God's great act of deliverance in the Exodus and strains forward in eschatological hope. Redemption is anchored in the death and resurrection of Jesus, but for struggling Christian congregations the fullness of resurrection remains on the horizon of a new age and a new church. As Paul says to the Romans, "For in hope we were saved. Now hope that is seen is not hope" (Rom. 8:24).

Finally, in Second Isaiah the agent of deliverance is not a powerful or supernatural figure but a servant who is diminished in every way (Isa. 42, 49–50, 52–53). Consider the Suffering Servant: the future of the church does not reside with rich, powerful, and successful organizations but among those with little power whose losses resemble those of the Servant and Savior himself.

In sum, the prophets of exile develop three themes applicable to any group of grieving believers: (1) they witness to the divine pathos, which is God's own empathy with their suffering; (2) they promise God's continued presence among the dislocated; (3) they imagine a restoration "with interest" (as Thomas Aquinas put it) that exceeds and transforms Israel's former condition of life. The bones of stricken congregations will come together again, but in a configuration no one can predict or engineer. It will be the Lord's work, as the restoration of exiles always is.

2. Diminished Congregations

The second mode of speech preachers may employ extends the prophetic witness and is found in the New Testament. It is the blessing of diminished churches. In the book of Revelation, the heavenly Son of Man says to the church at Philadelphia in Asia Minor: "I know that you have but little power, and yet you have kept my word and have not denied my name" (Rev. 3:8b). The speaker is addressing a church that is in a bad way. As a result of a massive earthquake decades earlier, the residents of Philadelphia were still living in tents. The apocalyptic imagery of Revelation 3 echoes Jesus' "Fear not, little flock, for it is your Father's good pleasure to give you the kingdom" (Luke 12:32 RSV). This and other passages reflect the "fear not" oracles of Second Isaiah: "Do not fear, for you will not be ashamed" (Isa. 54:4

and many others). These promises are gathered and stitched together in the words of the Sermon on the Mount spoken to the poor, persecuted, and meek. They are specifically formatted for the purpose of sustaining beleaguered congregations.

The encouragement addressed to small, divided, persecuted, or otherwise diminished congregations is a promise hidden in plain view throughout the New Testament. Many of Paul's letters are addressed to conflicted and harried house churches whose very survival is at stake. In 1 Peter the writer admonishes his addressees not to be surprised by the "fiery ordeal" that has come upon them (4:12). The evangelist Mark tells the story of chaos on the Sea of Galilee to a church decimated by Roman persecution (Mark 4:35–41).

This is to say, all too briefly, that there is a biblical word to be spoken to a church that is losing. In some cases, the message was first addressed to individuals and later applied to a larger body. In other cases, it originated in the cauldron of the church's struggle for survival and growth in a hostile culture.

3. Death and Resurrection

In either case, the preached word lives by the rhythm of Jesus, which is the rhythm of his death and resurrection. The New Testament is a sermon. The Gospel "memoirs," as Justin Martyr named them, provide none of the information we find indispensable in a modern memoir. Instead, they record an exteriorized account of "the events that have been fulfilled among us" (Luke 1:1) whose organizing principle is the proclamation of salvation in Jesus Christ. The primitive church filtered every datum about Jesus through its experience of his death and resurrection, giving to its holiest documents an arrow-like tendency toward death and new life.[9]

The church's rhythm of existence is governed by a rule that Jeremiah, Ezekiel, and Isaiah followed. The Apostle Paul and the evangelists followed it, too: one must die in order to rise again. "Unless a grain of wheat falls into the earth and dies, it remains just a single grain; but if it dies, it bears much fruit" (John 12:24). That is not a generic law of nature or history but the story of Jesus. Jesus had to die in order that God's justice could be vindicated by raising him from the dead. Superficially, our culture affirms the dialectic of death and resurrection in popular form: "No pain, no gain." "It's always darkest before the dawn." And so on. The biblical tradition, however, has longer legs and sharper vision. For it proclaims the dialectic's communal dimensions with reference to Israel, church, kinship, and cosmos. God's way with Israel and Jesus has become the way of the world. Individual congregations as well as our conventional notions of "church" must die. Like Jesus, they will rise and reappear, but in settings and shapes we have not imagined.

The event of death and resurrection has an immediate consequence, and it is mission. The risen Christ is a sending Lord, dispatching his followers to Galilee and to the ends of the earth. Those who have joined their lives to his follow the same trajectory with the same purpose. Latter-day disciples who have lost "church" as they once knew it are the seeds of the new thing God is doing. Like the once-dispirited witnesses to Jesus' death, they are missionaries to others who are bereft of church.

What, then, is the larger story that makes sense of our corporate experience of church? In terms of contemporary culture, much of the evidence points to a sea change in religious attitudes and a corresponding diminishment of church. But the familiar statistics and tales of woe do not constitute a grand narrative of loss. The umbrella narrative is ultimately not one of ecclesial slippage but the freedom of God to go into uncharted places and to create new realities. God goes with us into the strange new world of exile. And in that same, strange land, God promises to act in new and unanticipated ways. The Seer has already seen it: a new heaven and a new earth in the Last Days. In the meantime, fellow exiles, let's keep our eyes peeled for a new church.

PART IV   Church and Culture

Chapter 9

Learning From and Transforming the Community-Building Promise of Social Networking Services

Today's media culture is presenting new challenges for preaching. How do we preach effectively to a people who are used to sound bites, Twitter, and a visual entertainment culture? How do we preach about and help create genuine Christian community in a social networking culture?

*I*n his essay "Out of the Loop: The Changing Practice of Preaching,"[1] Tom Long argues that in a high-tech world, it is difficult to construct well-formed personal, life narratives. After reviewing Galen Strawson's work on "episodic" personal identities,[2] Long is convinced "that there are many people who experience life in a profoundly episodic fashion."[3] The reason for this, he concludes, is that "we are under cultural pressure to live life in random bursts, our attention fleeting from *American Idol* to troop movements in the Middle East to the desire to purchase a more desirable cell phone, a kind of cultural attention deficit disorder."[4] He goes on to show that, for many preachers, this means abandoning narrative-shaped models of preaching and migrating to a form of preaching that resembles hyperlinking between web pages or, in his words, "six points and a video clip."[5] Long argues that preaching in the next generation will need to reteach narrative competence itself and focus that competence on forming communities shaped more by the biblical narrative than by the notifications peppering the touchscreens of smartphones.

The present essay picks up, to some extent, where "Out of the Loop" ends. I want to highlight several ways in which worship and preaching within local communities of faith can both benefit from and transform key community-building elements within social networking services (hereafter SNS) in order to form genuine gospel-narrative-shaped Christian communities. Elsewhere, I have indicated that I am appreciative of many dialogical and inventive elements of what I have called a "mashup" culture.[6] What is required, how-ever, is a constructive rhythm between the networks and flows of online culture and "nodes of complexity" such as local congregations.[7] I am convinced that if preaching and worship are done well, local congregations at worship learn forms of participation, empathy, memory, content, and missional negotiation that are very much needed in order to create and sustain Christian communities with sufficient spiritual depth, biblical grounding, and theological complexity to thrive within the episodic flows of online culture.

1. From Logging In to Attendance

All communities assume some level of participation. There can be no community, by definition, unless there is consistent and regular involvement by a number of people. At the heart of any definition of community is the often-unsettling and disruptive business of "communing," that is, the business of allowing our lives to be interrupted and engaged by others in a common space (whether that space is physical or virtual). Most of us are involved in many different communities at any given time, which means that our lives are interrupted by many types of communal participation.

Participation involves *presence-with*. In the online world, this means, at the very least, sitting down at a computer or taking out one's smartphone, going online, and logging in to an online community or social network. Once logged in, we assume a role, or set of roles, within various online communities.

Communication theorists sometimes talk about "role-taking" and "role-playing" as crucial to becoming fully present with others in any community. In order to get to know someone, we "take" a role for them, initially a very obvious role (man, woman, father, mother, churchgoer, activist, fan, etc.), and then we "play" a commensurate role that suits us.[8] As we talk, these roles adjust and shift and we get to know more about where the person comes from, what they do, what they enjoy, and so on. We hope that the roles that are opened to us by another person are, as much as possible, congruent with some sort of "self" (or community of inner selves) and that we can trust these roles and the person behind them as a part of the overall fabric of the particular community in which we participate. At the same time, we realize that not every role that a person plays in life will necessarily show up in every community of participation.

Early forms of social networking (chat rooms, bulletin boards, etc.) tended to promote anonymity and identity-play online. Initially, this activity raised questions for some about whether the risks and consequences associated with "real-world" communities were possible in cyberspace.[9] Web 2.0 SNS such as Facebook, LinkedIn, and Google+, however, have done much to turn online communities into places where everyday identities are shared and in which real-world risks and consequences can be found (as those who have tried to erase online identities have discovered). Some have complained that social networks constrict communal participation to "narrowcast"[10] role-playing and that SNS force participants to conform to predetermined app-specific categories and roles (friend, favorite, follower, subscriber, commenter, etc.).[11] It is clear, however, that in many instances social media are helpful for enabling and broadening role-taking and role-playing dynamics, often bringing more authentic presence to bear in real-world relationships. For instance, Facebook time lines, while often edited, allow friends to view online histories (in photos, posts, and comments) in a way that broadens and deepens what participants might otherwise know about one another. At the same time, it is possible that social networks also allow those within one's network to see some of the other communities, both online and real-world, in which participants are involved.

Logging in to groups or conversations on SNS can play an important part in the development of energetic participation in Christian communities. By logging in to such groups or conversations, we learn to share religious identities and personal histories and to take risks in religious self-expression. At the same time, we experience ourselves, either consciously or unconsciously, taking roles for others and for God that are congruent with those in an online community as they engage religious ideas, issues, and problems. In online communities we allow ourselves to be interrupted by friends, followers, group members, and subscribers: uprooted from our daily lives and bound together with a common sense of identity and purpose. Logging in, therefore, provides a significant foretaste of genuine Christian community.

Christian worship in local congregations and communities of worship transforms the religious self-expression, role-taking, and role-playing experienced in SNS through a very different kind of participation: *attendance*. At first sight, "attendance" seems like a rather innocuous term implying doing one's duty—as in "perfect attendance" or "signing in." The deeper substratum of this term, however, might be found in such terms as "arriving," "showing up," "being physically present," "gathering with," "being fully available"—applying all our conscious faculties of observation and powers of participation, "answering a summons," and "waiting in anticipation and expectation that we will be rendered a service."

The business of becoming "fully present" in worship is a two-way affair. We gather to be fully present *with one another*, bringing to bear all our conscious powers of attention, and *with God,* who has summoned us together and promised to provide us with new life in Christ. This means that liturgists and preachers need to think carefully about the role-taking dynamics in worship and preaching. Worship leaders are those who "take" roles for God, indicating who it is that has summoned us and what, in fact, God promises. And worship leaders also invite participants to "play" roles in response—focusing our attention and garnering all our capabilities to become fully present and available—filled with anticipation. It is primarily biblical roles that guide this role-taking process: God as judge, healer, savior, liberator, mother hen, parent, and so on. Through these roles we hope to become present to one another in ways that respond to *who we are with God*, and the more expansive and congruent these roles are to the biblical narrative, the more fully present we are with one another in genuine Christian community.

In worship, however, another important dynamic pushes beyond role-taking and role-playing dynamics altogether. Worship invites participants on a journey beyond all roles into a place that is as transparent as possible before God and one another. Over the centuries praying prayers of confession, sitting on anxious benches, kneeling or bowing before God, and taking other actions all have expressed our awareness that before God, "attendance"—the presence of our true selves, "just as we are, without one plea"—is crucial to genuine Christian community. We hope to confess and, if possible, to strip away those things that keep us from "attending," from being fully present before God.

At the same time, we know that the roles we take for God, which are derived largely from human experience, are themselves inadequate to give full expression to God's own "attendance" in worship—to the fullness of who God is. Because we long for that fullness, we are moved to doxology, to praise. And so we exclaim, "You alone are holy," "Holy, holy, holy," or, in some churches, "Our God is an awesome God!"

Christian community, as it is developed through attendance within local congregations at worship, includes the desire to become fully and to some extent transparently *present* with one another and with God, and to invite God to be as richly and fully present with us as possible. Logging in to SNS groups and conversations has the potential to energize participation, identity-sharing, and role-taking that takes us to the threshold of this experience. Christian worship, then, focuses and extends role-taking and role-playing so that both human and divine participants "attend" in the deepest and most profound sense of the term.

2. From Empathy to Intercession

The best communities are those in which participants develop good listening skills. As we get to know one another, experimenting with role-taking and role-playing, we are sometimes able to move out beyond ourselves, to some extent, and "into someone else's shoes." This empathic ability helps us to have at least some glimmer of what the world looks like from another person's vantage point. Empathy is nearly impossible if we are always speaking or talking. It requires careful, deep listening and silence—the kind of listening silence that Nelle Morton once called "hearing into speech."[12] There need to be places of empathic listening within every community where all people can participate, give voice to their own struggles, celebrations, and interests, and experience themselves as having some real value to the community itself.

Across most SNS, empathy is framed in terms of "friendship," whether those friendships are professional (LinkedIn), with celebrities or informants (Twitter), or among personal contacts and groups of interest (Facebook). Some have worried that making empathic online connections distracts from real-world listening. Sherry Turkle, for instance, observes that obsession with checking one's smartphone is creating a culture in which we are "alone together."[13] Others argue that it is not empathy at all, but voyeurism that drives listening within online communities.[14]

In spite of these concerns, it is clear that social networks are quick to disseminate information about human needs, and response to those needs can be enhanced in a variety of ways through online interaction. The quality of this kind of empathic online contact is debatable, but it is clearly one of the key elements of online communication, whether it consists of congratulating someone on a new job on LinkedIn or sending words of comfort to someone who has lost a loved one or pet on Facebook. Although issues regarding privacy and confidentiality remain, as do issues around how to approach the Facebook page of persons who are deceased,[15] SNS are potentially conduits for increasing empathy and listening within online communities and beyond.

In Christian worship this kind of empathic listening is transformed and becomes "intercessory" in nature. In the community at prayer, God is present, hearing our deepest selves and our deepest needs, into speech. Intercessory prayers (sometimes called the "prayers of the people") have provided the gathered community of Christians over the centuries the opportunity to join with God and to engage in a kind of empathic listening that "intercedes" or "goes between" God and humanity.

Intercessory prayer protects empathy from disintegrating into identification—the assumption that we can *actually* stand in another's shoes, knowing their thoughts and feelings completely. By acknowledging that it is only God who knows these things, intercession protects the "otherness" of those around us in Christian community. Intercession joins us to *God's* empathy, God's immediate listening to the deepest desires of our hearts within the gathered community (what Paul calls the "sighs of the Spirit" in Rom. 8:26).

Empathic listening, necessary for the formation of genuine Christian community, is deepened and transformed by intercessory listening in Christian worship. Although some elements of intercession are possible within SNS (indicating that one is praying for someone, or actually posting a prayer), in local communities at worship we enter into the full communal posture of intercessors who partake not only in human empathy but in the divine empathy as well.[16]

3. From Archive to Anamnesis

Most communities cultivate some kind of memory, whether it takes the form of official narratives, time lines, scrolling (or actual scrolls), enacted rituals, or legends. Through memory (and the accumulation of memories) a community funds the present moment in time from a repository of beliefs, teachings, key defining events, and accumulated self-representations, all of which clarify the community's identity and purpose. Within social media, memory takes an *archival* shape—memory is "stored," given over to "the cloud" as archive or place of storage. On Facebook, for instance, "time lines" preserve personal memories, photographs, fleeting and permanent interests, meaningful and frivolous posts, fandoms old and new, conversations, and commentary. In blogs, online personalities archive personal or communal insights, daily reflections and perspectives, instructions, or narratives. On Instagram, photographs archive episodes in a life or community. On Twitter, celebrities and audiences create an archive of interactions, shared links, and comments. YouTube videos chronicle experiences, movements, celebrity development, and cultural heritage.[17] These and other social media give us windows into the past of other people and cultures around the globe as well. It is also possible in online communities to engage in extensive genealogical research, building new and deeper connections between the past and the present.

SNS empower an instantaneous sharing of memories, heritage, and culture. They allow people to create and recreate their own pasts, shared traditions, and community memories. As Graham Fairclough points out, social media break down the walls of our museums and cultural repositories and invite "everyone to participate in [the past's] construction, encouraging openness not closure of interpretation and valuation."[18] In short, communal memory within SNS is now a crowdsourced affair. Those who participate realize that their legacies, both personal and communal, are their own responsibility and are being constructed in an online universe. If they want those legacies to be accurate and shaped in a way that meets their own needs and desires, or those of their communities, it is crucial that they participate in the process of digitally archiving their own personal lives and communal existence.

Christian community, shaped by the gospel story in worship and preaching, is a community of *sacred memory*. Liturgical scholars often call this special kind of sacred memory *anamnesis*, by which they mean a form of active, self-conscious, performed (and performative) memory designed to bring foundational, sacred events from the past alive again in each generation.[19] The formal anamnesis within the Eucharistic Prayer includes a sometimes lengthy listing of the mighty acts of God on behalf of the community over the course of thousands of years. In order to shape communal memory in worship, lections from the Holy Bible are read; lectionaries are sometimes followed; the church year is observed; biblical themes are appropriated in anthems, hymns, prayers, and sermons; the narrative of salvation is sung, recited, interpreted, and reinterpreted; rituals like baptism, the Lord's Supper, foot washing, laying on of hands, and anointing are lifted from biblical moorings and reenacted; and literary and rhetorical forms from the Bible like doxology, lament, confession, thanksgiving, and eschatological urgency are performed anew. Through these and other activities, the community participates in a profound communal memory shaped by the gospel story. This memory grounds common life in a larger community—the communion of saints.

Archival memory—the *storage* of the past, including the sacred past—is not unimportant in Christian worship. In worship the community's past is indeed "stored" and archived within media. Bibles, prayer books, hymnals, bulletins, and other print media do this work, as do audio and video recordings that are posted online or distributed in analog or digital formats. In worship and preaching, however, memory is configured not just as archival but also as *kerygmatic* and *mimetic*. The past arrives in worship and preaching through the act of naming and performing key sacred sounds, words, or images. These sacred signs function as kergymatic markers around which the past can be recalled and organized. The markers establish what rhetoricians would call the "topics" or *topoi* of faith. They rise up out of the biblical text and the community's past and stand on their own as holy words that generate heat of heart: "Hear, O Israel," "Choose life," "Do justice, love mercy, and walk humbly," "It is finished," "He is risen," "Take, eat, this is my body," "There is now, therefore, no condemnation." Such memory is bequeathed to the church from oral cultures that are older than the written word. In oral cultures, habits, customs, myths, legends, and traditions grow up around sacred words and images, and the past comes to life in the repetition and reperformance of those customs and traditions.[20]

Through this repetition in ritual and proclamation, the past also shapes memory as *mimesis*—the aesthetic imitation of a pattern or "ordo" that gives shape to memory. An ordo might place word next to table, praise next to beseeching, Lord's day next to workweek, Lent next to Easter, baptism next to water, and so on.[21] Sacred memory, therefore, is given a particular kind of patterning in worship and preaching—a patterning that recapitulates the sacred past in such a way that it lives anew in the present. In his Lyman Beecher lectures, *Preaching from Memory to Hope*,[22] Tom Long urges preachers to recover and deepen mimetic practices. He takes great care to show how important various forms of mimesis can be for reincorporating the past in preaching and worship. Through mimesis the past arrives anew.

Kerygmatic and mimetic forms of memory ultimately come together and assume a narrative shape. This narrative has its center in the life, death, and resurrection of Jesus Christ. Christian community cultivated in local communities gathered for worship and preaching grows out of this sacred memory. Anamnestic practices help rescript life according to a new biblical and theological pattern that reinterprets the past in light of new contexts and situations.

The immediate archiving of the world's experiences within social media has tremendous potential to intersect with the church's anamnesis of the life, death, and resurrection of Jesus. In particular, the archival memories of SNS can connect the church to marginalized experiences, and especially experiences of suffering in the world today. This occurred, for instance, in the testimonial and video archiving within social media of the human rights abuses perpetrated by Boko Haram in Nigeria and in the video archiving of the killing of Michael Brown in Ferguson, Missouri. Such archiving has the potential to support the church's anamnesis by helping to commemorate what Johann Baptist Metz calls the "dangerous memories" of suffering in the world that are closely related to the suffering of Jesus.[23] Such memories cannot, however, stand on their own. They cannot live only in fleeting online posts, blogs, or forums. In the gathered community committed to performing and reperforming the sacred past, the memories of all those now missing due to violence and victimization are nested within the narrative of the suffering of Jesus and brought before God for meaning and redemption.

Archives give concrete specificity to anamnesis; anamnesis raises the data of archives into songs of lament, stories of courage, hymns of thanksgiving, and prayers for redemption.

4. From Aspiration to Anticipation

Most communities, by definition, gather *around* something, some *content*— usually an ideal, task, topic, issue, celebrity, artist, or product. The same is true for communities cultivated with social media. Although some argue that SNS are more about promoting the *desire* for content, rather than creating "content communities,"[24] social media have proven to be invaluable for disseminating content on behalf of communities of common interest. Facebook updates, YouTube videos, and Twitter feeds can be extremely helpful for promoting and sharing content. Social activists and revolutionaries, for instance, make good use of social media to disseminate information, shape group opinion, and mobilize action. Many churches use social media in a similar way.

Although not all SNS content is oriented toward community building, media philosopher Patrick Stokes observes that much of the intentional community-oriented content within social media is "aspirational" in nature.[25] Aspirations are the things we direct our hopes and ambitions toward achieving. For instance, a person might share content produced by action groups for the homeless, a woman's shelter, a group demonstrating against capital punishment, and a local congregation involved in a street protest. Persons aspiring toward social justice will "like," "share," "retweet," or "favorite" such content. Many friends or followers may respond, indicating that an online community of aspiration exists. Sometimes members of this aspirational community will, in fact, donate funds or become actively involved in any or all these groups. The same will be true for many kinds of aspirational content: political agendas, products (and product placements), celebrity opinions, artistic insights, psychotherapeutic approaches, or weight loss programs.

Aspirational ideas and messages are not foreign to the gospel story. Jesus' disciples wanted to identify themselves with Jesus and aspired to achieve his mission. The gospel story, however, was forged in a unique kind of eschatological context, in which human aspirations are reshaped and fulfilled in new and unexpected ways by Christ. Because of this, the content of the Christian gospel transforms *aspirations* into *anticipations*. The content of Christian worship and preaching takes the form of a *promise*: the Reign of God has drawn near. This promise, as we noted in the previous section, is grounded in a bible-shaped sacred memory—in the inauguration of the Reign of God in the faith of Israel and in the person and work of Jesus Christ. This promise is also eschatological; it is future-directed and anticipates the transformation of all things by God in and through Jesus Christ.

While Christians direct our aspirations and ambitions toward the Reign of God, in worship our aspirations encounter the life, death, and resurrection of Christ and are changed into God's pledge, a mustard seed *already* in our midst that is *not yet* fully manifest. God who is already incarnate, already with us, transforms our aspirations into a very particular kind of eschatological anticipation of a God who is coming to us and so fulfilling promises made in the Incarnation. Through Word and Sacrament, Christ becomes incarnate, fully present, *already* alive in the community at worship. That presence is experienced as a pledge, a promise of what is *coming*. Worship performs that promise by incorporating people into it at the baptismal font, narrating it from the pulpit, and nurturing our bodies with it at the Lord's Table. Christian anticipation, therefore, already experiences the content of its hope—the Reign of God is experienced in the community at worship. We aspire to it; yet it has already been achieved by God and is coming again. Genuine Christian community shaped by liturgists and preachers, therefore, transforms human aspirations and gathers the community around *anticipatory,* or *promissory*, content.

5. From Messaging to Mission

All communities engage in the negotiation of ideas and action—two practices that are inevitably intertwined. Every community interprets the meaning and value of its interaction, including such things as its identity, purpose, goals, mission, reason for being, history, and place in the larger scheme of things. In light of this interpretation, a community will promote certain forms of action or reaction. Through its teaching ministry and preaching, Christian communities engage in responsible interpretive negotiations and decisions regarding who the church is and what it is to do in the world as the Body of Christ. While not necessarily a community of consensus, genuine Christian community functions as a community of *mission*.

One popular ideal today, at the heart of the so-called "missional church," is that "mission shapes the church" rather than "the church shapes mission."[26] This missional perspective offers a much-needed corrective to what Anglican theologian Christopher Duraisingh calls the "culture of membership" that devours so much energy in most congregations. Instead, missional theologians like Duraisingh encourage the church to key its inner life on its outer commitments—to work backward from its mission in the world to the development of its worship, education, and organization.[27] The millennial generation is applying this to the development of many alternative forms of church.

The mission-shaped church finds a natural home within SNS, where developing relationships, connections, friendships, and communities of aspiration online permit a message church, or rather a church-as-messaging, to thrive. In this context, the church exists in and as online communication. It *is* its missional identity, which is achieved by means of sharing substantially similar and interrelated mission messages. In some instances, elements of such mission can be both ecumenical and interfaith in appeal: saving the environment, overcoming economic justice, or eradicating homelessness.

There are many debates about whether SNS messaging increases participation in on-the-ground communities of action or, in fact, turns people away from political and social action. Those on the positive side of this debate argue that Facebook and Twitter played a significant role in the 2011 revolutions in Egypt and Tunisia.[28] Others fear that social media promote enclaves of like-minded individuals who tend to "unfriend" those who challenge their views.[29] Political philosopher Asaf Bar-Tura worries that hitting a "like" button may create a "false sense of activity and accomplishment" that engenders passivity in the public sphere.[30] At the same time, there is ample concern about the quality of information disseminated through social media and the polarized and often reactionary ideas that circulate with such power.[31]

In spite of these concerns, SNS promote an enormous range of information sharing. Participation in SNS guarantees confrontation with a broader range of perspectives on religious, social, and political issues than one is likely to have otherwise. The perspectives of religious personalities and thought leaders such as Brian McLaren, Pope Francis, Miroslav Volf, and Elaine Pagels are easily accessible through Facebook and Twitter. If nothing else, SNS make available more information and generate an increased negotiation among ideas and missional possibilities.

Christian communities formed in local congregations at worship have the possibility to become not only mission shaped but also mission-shaping.[32] Although hopefully shaped by the church's mission, worship and preaching do much to add depth, complexity, and guidance to those who are seeking to be part of this mission. Through education, preaching, contextual analysis, and self-reflection, Christian communities can test proposals for action, pool resources, and help to formulate clear, local plans of actions, either short term or long term, in order to further the work of God in the world. In worship, the relationship between Word and Sacrament seals the relationship between biblical interpretation and ethics and invites the entire community to engage in a similar interpretative and ethical praxis, actualizing its attendance, intercession, and memory in a gospel-shaped missional praxis.

The Rhythm between the Episodic and the Narratival

We have now identified five unique and important aspects of Christian community formation that are shaped by local congregations gathered for worship and preaching.

- *Attendance*: becoming fully present with one another and with God
- *Intercession*: immediate and simultaneous participation in the divine empathy
- *Anamnesis*: the *kerygmatic* and *mimetic* performance of sacred memory
- *Anticipation*: the palpable experience of the Reign of God *already* in our midst but *not yet* fully manifest
- *Mission*: discernment of and critical reflection on the mission of the church

The argument here is not that SNS and local worshipping communities are in an oppositional relationship. Rather, worship and preaching in local communities of faith can be helpfully informed by many of the community-building aspects of SNS.[33] At the same time, local worshipping communities regularly participate in rituals, practices, education, and mission that are much needed in order to transform the community-building aspects of SNS into elements of genuine Christian community. To couch this in terms used by Tom Long in his essay "Out of the Loop," there is the possibility of a vibrant rhythm between the "episodic" and the "narratival," and each of these qualities can be important to what it means to be in genuine Christian community today. As we have seen, the so-called episodic elements within SNS have the potential to broaden communal participation, crowdsource memory, connect people by means of aspirational content, and encourage congregations in their worship and preaching to be shaped more clearly and intentionally by particular missional objectives. These are all potentially helpful and even game-changing contributions to the formation of genuine Christian community.

Our argument here, however, is that, left to their own (technological) devices, these more episodic elements of community formation can become ephemeral and decentered to the point of lacking any clear orientation (except, of course, toward capital and power). In my opinion, Tom Long's entire body of work has been devoted to developing forms of preaching and worship that will attend carefully to the many ways that biblical texts both *come from* and are meant to *shape* communities of faith. He has never invited us to run away from the present and future but always to make sure that every generation of preaching and worship is grounded as richly and deeply as possible in the grand narrative of Abraham, Sarah, Joseph, Deborah, Mary, Jesus, Paul, and many others who, in developing their own personal narratives, attended with great care to the narrative conveyed to them through the worship and oral traditions of communication within their own local communities of faith.

Chapter 10

Prophetic Truth-Telling in a Season of Fatigue and Fragmentation

TERESA FRY BROWN

How do we preach prophetically in a seriously divided nation and world without being tuned out?

If we are fundamentally bored by what we are doing, feel contempt for or superior to the hearers, are cynical toward what we are preaching, try to be impressive or charming, or wish we were in some other vocation, that will also show. A person who, week after week, is speaking the truth in love looks and sounds like a person lovingly telling the truth; there is finally no hiding it.[1]

*P*reacher, professor, pastor, author, and mentor Thomas G. Long penned these words in 1989, yet they still ring true in the hearts, minds, and ears of twenty-first century preachers. Preaching can be an arduous mental and physical task, a fragile faith-directing influence, and an emotionally-charged responsibility. These realities affect each preacher differently. There are times the preacher or proclaimer senses the urgency of "telling the story" and "worshipping God in spirit and in truth" and cannot wait until Sunday morning to share the good news. There are other times when the preacher or proclaimer is too overburdened with pastoral duties, overwhelmed with family crises, or overextended with social, political, and community responsibilities to address the "issue of the week." Preaching can start to feel like a check-off box on a long list of pastoral duties.

These realities are always present for preachers. They are especially acute for "prophetic" preachers seeking social transformation. Often transformation comes slowly, if at all. The work can try the patience of even the most patient prophet. And it almost always arouses opposition that seeks to discredit, silence, or even destroy the preacher. People who try to speak prophetic words have a way of ending up in the wilderness.

126

Long issues a call to preach God's truth in love even in these moments of wilderness. "I think what we need to realize about the cycle of highs and lows in preaching," he writes,

> when they are experienced by a minister faithfully attempting to perform the ministry of preaching, is that they are an embodiment of the true nature of the Christian life. Week after week the people gather around the Word. What they hear sometimes is a preacher who vibrates with passion and excitement. What they hear other times is a preacher who is perplexed, dry as dust, struggling to get in touch with the vision, or trying to squeeze blood out of stone. That is the way with sermons, and that is the way it is with Christian life, too. The ups and downs of preaching are a ritual enactment of the rhythms of the Christian life. We find a powerful witness to the faith in a congregation who experiences their minster struggling with preaching, sometime having much and sometime having little. When the sermon is rich and full, it is a banquet of grace. When the sermon is less than that, it is still, like manna, enough to go on.[2]

Long knows that contemporary preachers encounter a variety of emotional, psychological, social, cultural, political, and denominational factors that at times leave them searching for fresh manna. Sometimes these factors are personal. Preachers might be "faithfully attempting to perform the ministry of preaching" yet find themselves confronted with instantaneous comparisons of their style, content, voice, and mannerisms with those of others that their hearers have heard in person or through some media. And sometimes the factors driving preachers into the wilderness are more systemic. A constant digital diet of global and domestic wars, terrorism, mass murders, conspiracy theories, organized crime, gang violence, natural disasters, gender discrimination, immigration challenges, racial profiling, denominational turf wars, generational differences, declining memberships, domestic violence, bullying, economic and educational disparities, legal inequalities, and global prejudice can all come together to produce what I have come to call "justice fatigue."[3]

Preachers still seek to share a word of hope with those who weekly "gather around the Word" in spite of the personal and systemic challenges they are facing. While some congregations understand that a preacher's humanity and spirituality grow as the preacher grows, others hold expectations that the preacher already has all of life's questions solved, constantly walks closely with God, is a bottomless reserve of biblical knowledge, and preaches sermons that need no preparation. The standards are untenable, yet preachers still sense the pressure to be pastoral and prophetic at all times.

Given the complexities of preaching in the twenty-first century, it is predictable that one of the questions posed by both experienced and novice preachers is: How does one preach prophetically in a seriously divided nation and world without being tuned out? How can prophetic preachers connect the times Long describes as "dry as dust," when they are "struggling to squeeze blood out of stone," to the times when they "vibrate with passion and excitement"? This essay briefly will explore contemporary challenges associated with prophetic preaching in relation to the following topics: the call to preach prophetic sermons, the role of the Bible in sustaining contextual transformative preaching, the need to ascertain one's preaching context, the challenge of finding the appropriate prophetic voice and language, and the justice fatigue that can set in during a season of fragmentation.

The Call of the Prophet

German sociologist, philosopher, and political economist Karl Emil Maximilian "Max" Weber defined a prophet as an agent of radical social change, a charismatic figure claiming a personal, divine call to act.[4] This designation has had great power in shaping imaginations of what a prophetic preacher needs to be. But it can be burdensome for preachers. It makes prophetic work a dynamic, cutting-edge, activist job specification above and beyond pastoral duties. It suggests a person who speaks evocative and provocative truths. It also relegates the preacher to becoming a conduit of God's instructions for the people.

Moreover, Weber's definition forgets that being prophetic means not only speaking out against the evil of others but also holding the mirror up to our own lives. Prophets are called to do more than console and answer questions. Prophets persuade listeners to accept the power God gives them to implement changes in their lives and in the world around them. Prophets are nonconformists.

As Steven Long has written, "The prophetic preacher stands under the community of faith; he or she is not set over and against it. . . . Prophetic preaching is never discontinuous with the past but finds resources internal to the tradition of the community of faith to call that community to its true identity."[5] Prophets assist their listeners with the identification, examination, and resolution of alienation, conflict, and oppression that is located both within the biblical text and within society. Telling and retelling stories of salvific incidents of God's self-revelation, action, and promises in human history is the deep, emotional work of prophets.

Answering the call to become a preaching prophet may be life-giving, but it may also prove death-dealing, particularly when there is no respite from prophetic utterances. Living, preaching, and working under the prophetic call may impact the ability of some preachers to address topics relevant to the particular lived experiences of their congregations. The pressures of prophetic witness may tempt some to resort to plagiarism or take short cuts in their exploration of the biblical text. Others may gradually abdicate their prophetic edge in favor of a reinforced status quo of silence. The call to prophetic preaching is a call to vulnerability.

Thankfully, that call is not just to individuals. Preaching prophetically has individual dimensions, but it is also a communal and even global endeavor. For true prophetic preaching does not grow out of a single preacher's agenda but out of biblical imperatives regarding humanity and just practices.

Manna for Preaching: The Role of the Bible in Sustaining Contextual Transformative Preaching

The duty of the preacher is to address the relevant needs of the listeners in ways that are grounded in the biblical text and the transforming message of Jesus and that expand to affirm the humanity of all persons. Immersing oneself in the biblical text as preparation for preaching will relieve pressure on prophetic preachers, especially those searching for twenty-first-century topics. From Genesis to Revelation, the Bible provides depth for prophetic utterances. Prophetic preaching, however, is more than the reiteration of Micah 6:6–8 or Luke 4:18–19. The entire biblical text is manna, spiritual sustenance, instructions, and commandments for how humans are to be present with God and each other. Lack of biblical engagement may lead one to preach a privatized "gospel according to myself" that relies on an exclusionary and hate-filled hermeneutic.

Tom Long shared his thoughts on the importance of the Bible for prophetic preaching during an interview on Luther Seminary's "Working Preacher" website. "If a preacher never is surprised by the biblical witness in relationship to his or her own political views," Long said, "then your God is too small and your Bible is too small. You're looking at the Bible as an endorsement of your political agenda."[6] There is an immeasurable number of so-called prophetic sermons that emanate from a preacher's narrow focus rather than the fullness of the biblical witness. Long advises that the preacher should "allow a text from the Bible to serve as the leading force in shaping the content and purpose of the sermon" and should engage in "telling the truth about—bearing witness to—what happens when a biblical text intersects some aspect of our life and exerts a claim upon us."[7] Preachers should call on the collective memory embodied in the selected text, repurposing the text to engage the needs of the community and the purposes of the sermon.

A preacher who reads the entire text instead of just a few snippets, who explores multiple translations, who walks around in the life of the text, and who is able to make connections to the text through observation of the lived experiences of the local congregation and the surrounding culture may be able to add prophetic preaching to his or her spiritual resume. The biblical text speaks of being transformed by the renewing of our minds, and biblical manna assists preachers in the process of deprogramming our thoughts about self and others, engaging institutions, social structures, and persons who seek to enslave us, and imagining new and different ways of living as God created people in God's created world.

Tom Long also reminds us of the transformation that should take place within the preacher when wrestling with biblical texts:

> If you never get more generous toward people that you think are wrong, if you never get more illumination on an issue about which you are sure you are right, if you never get forced to your knees in repentance over a position you have taken, you probably aren't engaging the Scripture faithfully on these issues.[8]

Ascertaining Preaching Contexts

Knowing one's preaching context is another consideration for avoiding burnout, the loss of cutting-edge rhetoric, and the cooptation of one's activist commitments. Theologian W. Paul Jones wrote that the truth of one's faith perspective as a Christian is its "livability, tested in the midst of a supportive and accountable faith community."[9] The community is so important that the preacher needs to be aware of the composition of the listening congregation. The demographics—age, education, income, political stance, gender, sexuality, ethnicity—as well as the social location, activist tendencies, and history of those poised to receive the preached word are all essential to the efficacy of the sermon. What is the cultural composition of the congregation? Persons of like ethnicities, values, denominations, ages, and beliefs are often more accepting of a preacher who is like them than one who is distinctively different. What types of listeners are in the congregation? Emphatic listening provides maximum understanding of the speaker's intent and content. The listener evaluates through deliberative or selective listening. The emphatic listeners recall critical issues, agreements, or disagreements with the speaker and draw conclusions. The deliberative listeners may have minimal understanding or are predisposed to criticize, summarize, conclude, agree, or disagree.[10] All these factors and more should be considered for a thorough understanding of the context of the congregation.

Preachers may also need to undergo a bit of self-evaluation in order to glean how relevant they are. How do members of the congregation respond during the preaching moment? How does the preacher know if or when the congregation understands the sermon? How does the preacher handle criticism and praise? Issues of power, authority, and culture affect the preacher's understanding of how well she or he is preaching.

There are specific expectations regarding preaching style and content in diverse settings. Women are sometimes termed speakers rather than preachers. There may be an expectation that white males are scholarly and boring, Korean men are deeply reverent, and black males are emotional and loud. Each may be preaching a prophetic message, but listener feedback, rejection, or acceptance may lead them to co-opt their substantive information for another style of delivery. Due to pervasive digital access to preaching, the congregation may have heard the selected text or title before. Their attention to what is being said may be related to what they heard prior to coming to service. Stylistic differences in presentation of the Word—in sound, pronunciation, volume, animation, and bodily movement—influence both the messenger and the reception of the messenger. Power and authority disparities between the preacher and the congregation often hamper both the preacher's ability to speak and the congregation's ability to hear the sermon. Preconceived notions about the preacher's oratorical skill, reputation, personhood, or faith at times obscure the communication channel. Static in the communication channel may emanate from the language meanings or type of language used in the tradition, by the preacher, or in the other elements of worship. The preacher has little power to control some of these factors. Others are more easily handled.

Preachers should ask ourselves if our preaching is transportable. Do we preach differently in different cultural contexts? Preachers juggling more than one service, church, congregation, or multiple outside speaking or conference engagements need to evaluate the distinctive nature of each preaching space before the preaching moment. Modification of introductory approach to the sermon, text, content, illustrations, and delivery style may be warranted. The truth of the text, however, remains the same.

The late pastor, activist, and preacher par excellence Samuel Dewitt Proctor once said, "Speaking the truth in love, at least in some cultural contexts, is a foundational principle of preaching. . . . Some pastors have given up on filling the shoes of Amos, Micah, Isaiah, or Jeremiah. . . . God bless those pastors who stand tall and who, in love, tell the truth."[11] I would add that in some cultural contexts, speaking the truth in love is a death knell for preachers. We live in an era of entertainment preaching that promises wealth with little responsibility and uses music to cajole listeners into the kingdom. The truth of the matter is that many congregants are detached from social issues and remain misinformed regarding the meaning of "separation of church and state." They believe preachers should never address any social ill. Those who would be prophetic preachers need to understand these features of their contexts.

The listeners' understanding of why and how the preacher delivers a message of prophecy is intricately linked to how the preacher begins and continues to compose and share cutting-edge messages. The congregation and preacher must know that the goal of the preaching transformation is to rescue humanity from the grip of slow death while pricking our individual and collective consciences to move toward a change in thought, behavior, method, emotion, ability, or action.

Choose Your Words Wisely

The preacher must share that the message is not the intellectual property, morning musings, or retaliatory rhetoric of the preacher but an assignment to verbally affirm God's directives for humanity. The prophetic call to justice is not based on guilt, moralism, or misguided obedience to a principle of political correctness but on a joyful, festive response to the in-breaking of God's future. God's in-breaking is an act of kairos that interrupts the flow of chronos-time. Too often transformation or change becomes a legislative act, a "by any means necessary" mantra, or a "with all deliberate speed" mandate rather than a God-ordained imperative.

Preaching is an opportunity to use God's gift of language to its fullest. Words affect the heart, soul, and mind. The preacher's transformative voice is essential to ending divisiveness. In order for a preacher to speak with metamorphic boldness he or she must own the uniqueness of voice. The preacher must be committed to oral communication, keeping words simple, clear, and appropriate. One must invite the listeners, both as individuals and as a community, into self-examination and fuller personal engagement with the biblical text. The preacher must relay hope for change, looking from present realities to future possibilities. Finally, the preacher must lead the community in celebration of what God has done, is doing, and will do in their lives.

The preacher seeks to use language to open up means for all of God's children to stand on equal footing, which by necessity involves the critique of inequities in interpersonal relationships, families, communities, churches, and in the world. Exclusionary language that denies full personhood to women, children, elders, LGBTQI persons, the poor, the houseless, or the disabled is alive and well in preaching. Prophetic preachers will find better words.

At times, those who are supposed to speak about love and power perpetuate an ethos of "*in-powerment*," a word I have coined to describe the dynamic in which those who have power dictate what is acceptable language. The social-political nature of language means that those with actual power dictate standards of academic/intellectual language, what is "proper" language, what meanings/descriptors are approved, or whose sentence/grammatical structures are correct. The people holding perceived power then use these factors to define the intelligence and expertise of the preacher. Those who are not privileged to know the "in language" or "Theo-speak" are unable to understand or deliver sermonic material in ways that are approved. These power dynamics are inculcated by one group in order to control or limit another's participation in the communicative encounter. A cognitive dissonance sets up, for example, when a preacher addresses the topic of equality in the Reign of God while using derogatory or oppressive language that subordinates some group.

Language is power. Meaning-making in the preaching moment may be hampered by conflicting theologies, choice of topics, imagery, and illustrations. Effective communication in the preaching moment is grounded in cohesion. Both sides of the transmission know the forms and conventions of language. This facilitates a participatory, inviting interchange between the preacher as oral interpreter of the written text and the people as cultural interpreters of the message. This is the intentionality of preaching that leads to a fuller reception, association, contemplation, assimilation, and transformation in the lives of the preacher and listener of the preached word.

Preachers also have an ability to filter language to make it more contextually powerful. Some explore the creation of new, refreshed, or remixed concepts to explain prophetic points. Some omit hot-button issues or buzzwords that cause sermonic embolism or disdain from congregants. Some resort to euphemisms, humor, or linguistic subtleties to introduce difficult topics more gradually. Regardless of one's homiletical strategy, prophetic rhetoric is not individual; it is communal. Selected words and phrases are for the benefit, action, and purposes of the entire community, not just the preacher. Adapting Molefi Kete Asante's work on rhetoric, each prophetic sermon involves a rhetoric of resistance to and struggle against forces that stifle the liberation and freedom promised in the biblical text. The preacher is charged to employ a rhetoric of affirmation that affirms the status, personhood, right to be free, right to a meaningful life, and social-historical responsibilities of each listener. The result of prophetic utterance is to develop a rhetoric of possibility or increased persuasion to enable the listener to share information and search and explore possibilities in the social and human condition.[12]

Finding a Voice for Transformational Preaching

The job specification of a prophetic preacher is multifaceted. It can be draining if one attempts to be the "voice crying in the wilderness," wearing coordinated sackcloth and ashes continually. If a pastor sets out to preach prophetic sermons every Sunday, be present at every protest, write all the dissenting e-mails, or rage against the established institutions at every opportunity, he or she will implode. If a preacher believes she or he is the only one living with the burden of social change, then burnout is likely.

It takes time to develop a prophetic voice. Prophetic voice is intrapersonal and interpersonal. It is not stagnant but dynamic. The prophetic voice engages call and response. The community answers the call of the preacher. The preacher responds to the needs and abilities of the community. Once the community trusts the prophetic preacher, the preaching voice becomes clear and convincing even when the circumstances demand that the voice become loud and agitated.

The prophetic voice must invite the listeners, both as individuals and as a community, into self-examination and fuller personal engagement with the biblical text. The prophetic voice seeks to address what is deemed to be not of God and points persons toward life-changing decisions.

Foundational to transformational preaching or speaking truth to power is proficiency with sermonic language. The sermon is not just a theoretical exercise in biblical scholarship but also a practical, day-in day-out application of faith to a particular situation.[13] Relevant preachers must speak to the hungers of all people who sit in the pews—not just economic hungers but also hungers for freedom. All people need a sense of place, roots, and history.

Sermons are to effect behavioral change through conversion, discipleship, forgiveness, honesty, generosity, and humility. The purpose of the prophetic sermon is to transform the preacher and the congregation. The transformational voice avoids pop psychology-based sermons and group counseling from the pulpit that leave more persons in pain after the "living word" than before. The "just have faith," "tell your story now," "just get over it," "it wasn't that bad," "it is all your fault" mantras of many contemporary preachers are unhelpful at best and dangerous at worst. The transformational voice addresses the lived experiences of all those people, places, and things that experience exploitation, marginalization, powerlessness, and imperialism. Such sermons offer the hopeful expectation of the eradication of these conditions rather than vague promises of material gain.

The transformational voice does not spout cheap grace or a quick fix but patient endurance, anticipation, and confidence that the end of the matter is at hand, accomplished not yet but soon. The transformational voice also speaks truth to power. It works to end practices that establish, maintain, and perpetuate subordination, exploitation, marginalization, powerlessness, cultural imperialism, "othering," systematic violence, and the subjugation of the knowledge possessed by people on the margins of society. Such preaching points to the fire on the outside of the cave, the light of truth, and calls God's people to pursue religious and social questions and issues that affect all God's family. In *Luminous Darkness* Howard Thurman asks us to imagine a time and place when we reject stereotypes, report prejudice, and do justice.[14] The *ability to speak truth to power* should never be taken for granted regardless of who seeks to silence the masses.

In short, the job specification for a prophetic preacher is to be a holistic communicator who engages the spiritual, intellectual, social, psychological, and economical yearnings and needs of all people. This includes the person preaching the sermon. In an age replete with vivid media, shorter attention spans, and a maturing population, the preacher's prophetic voice must speak the language of transformation, not status quo.

Prophetic Truth-Telling in a Season of Fatigue and Fragmentation

A perpetual question for seasoned and novice preachers centers around how one faithfully proclaims God's lifesaving Word in a changing, confusing, and callous world. Preachers have historically encountered nonbelievers, declining church membership, hostile communities, questions of faith, and inhuman pastoral work schedules. The twenty-first century retains these challenges and adds more. There are blurred lines between political and religious beliefs so that in some spaces the claim that "God is no respecter of persons" is trumped by "my Bible says" that a particular group is inhuman or hell-bound. The cult of celebrity means the first line of truth even for people of faith is a person who may or may not be a follower of Christ. Cyberchurch (playing out on Twitter, Facebook, YouTube, Instagram, and other platforms) opens the way for instant viewing, support, attack, critique, and defamation of preachers. So-called experts on reality television, blogs, and social media distort life and issues the preacher may seek to address. Congregational fact-checking and "Googling God" during the sermon adds anxiety, second-guessing, and deferral of hard truths on the part of the preacher. Dehumanization of other faith systems and ignorance of diverse cultures are common.

All these factors can produce weariness in preachers. And the pursuit of justice can be especially exhausting. Social justice fatigue can have many sources. It can arise from an occasion when preachers find the situation hopeless. It can also arise from the congregation, when it becomes apparent that the congregation wishes to be spoon-fed activism. And it can arise from outside the congregation, as denominations, other institutions, and even friends press the pastor to avoid any sociopolitical engagement.

Strategies for Prophetic Truth-Telling

There is an Akan word from Ghana, *Sankofa*, meaning to go back and get, to snatch, to remember what came before. I would propose that contemporary cave-dwelling, justice-fatigued, still dreaming, cautiously hopeful preachers take time to seek the lessons of those who came before us. There is no need to reinvent the wheel. It is time to use our own tools to strategize in our own particular contexts. No matter how much technology we use or how many studies say we live in an inclusive and just society, there is a need for prophetic voices to ensure that all aspects of life are accessible to every person. The justice journey is fraught with difficulty and danger. Metamorphic boldness is needed to walk it. These suggestions for "walking it" stem from my writings and presentations on a womanist homiletic.[15]

> 1. *Radical subjectivity* involves doing faith work even in the face of resistance, denial, and ostracism. The preacher speaks the truth in love even in the face of an oppressor. She or he raises the consciousness of the listeners about the possibilities of liberation and justice for all persons, not only in word, but also in deed, regardless of the individual or communal cost.[16]
> 2. *Traditional communalism* is a belief that God intends us to be free and assists us and empowers us in the struggle for freedom. The preacher proactively addresses the complex structures that homiletician Christine Smith has called "webs" of oppression.[17] Smith lists forces like exploitation ("the systemic transfer of benefits from one person to the advantage

of another"), marginalization ("the unwillingness or inability of an economic system to use the capabilities of a person or group of persons"), powerlessness ("the position of being the recipient of directions of others but unable to give orders or exercise control over one's situation"), cultural imperialism ("the universalization of one culture to the exclusion of others"), and violence ("the dimension of institutionalized or socially permissible violence against persons or groups").[18]

3. *Redemptive self-love* is the celebration and affirmation of self-care and love of humanity. It is a form of agency, a decision to seize the day. *Carpe diem*! It means each of us is responsible for our own healing, getting up off the mat, getting our own water, and speaking our own minds without allowing others to put words in our mouths or hijack our thoughts or silence our beliefs. Survival and thriving in the world is possible through the practice of self-love. Self-love means knowledge of and appreciation for one's own personhood regardless of outside critique or societal standards. Preachers need to remember they are human and need to honor their own convictions and emotions.

4. *Critical engagement* means one strives to learn from as many different people as one can. Critical engagement is a means to imaginatively examine life as we know it. Life may not make sense. Mining the deep in the biblical text and in one's own beliefs, even when one is suffering from disappointment in humanity, is imperative.

5. *Appropriation and reciprocity* means utilizing a form of spirit-love as one turns to the wisdom of the elders, identifying community sayings and lived moral wisdom that keep one grounded and full of hope in the face of social constrictions. Preachers need to be reminded that they are not the first or the last to deal with a particular social issue. One cannot solve a personal, community, or world's problem in one sermon or sermon series.

One or all these considerations may prove helpful as one contemplates what it means to preach prophetically in a divided nation and world without being tuned out. A summative piece of advice from Tom Long's pen answers this query succinctly: "In responsible preaching there is simply no substitute for reading, thinking, reflecting, exploring, gathering, digging, watching, and analyzing. No one preaches with ease."[19]

The challenge of contemporary prophetic preaching, when done correctly, is momentous. The preacher may need to take time to review her or his call, textual integrity, context, beliefs, voice, and resources. It will not be easy. One may want to give up, but it is possible to go on.

PART V   Hopeful Signs

Chapter 11

Tomorrow's Breaking News

The Horizon of North American Preaching

SALLY A. BROWN

*Where on the national scene do we in the United States find signs of
hope regarding preaching today? What can we learn about preaching from the new things the Holy Spirit is doing in our midst?*

Ask about signs of hope, and you have flung open the door to ambiguity. To
a five-year-old boy, the toy store across the parking lot crammed to the ceil-
ing with things that light up, clang, and shoot projectiles is a sign of hope. To
his grandparents, his custodians for the weekend, it's the hand-lettered sign
posted on the door of the place that signals hope: "Closed until Monday."
Whether the landscape we're talking about is the global economy, this weekend's weather forecast, or preaching in North America, what counts as a sign
of hope depends on what we value.

Mapping the North American Homiletical Landscape

Christian preaching in North America is a wide-ranging, multiform, and constantly shifting phenomenon. This makes any attempt at brief assessment
necessarily incomplete. This limitation is compounded by the ephemeral
nature of preaching as an event of speaking and hearing. Many more sermons are captured digitally than in print these days; yet the vast majority of
sermons take place in small and scattered places of worship, urban and rural,
leaving no trace in either the print or the digital universe.

Imagine, then, that we have stepped off a plane in a large North American city with the aim of spending several weeks sampling the preaching
going on in its downtown neighborhoods, its exurbs and suburbs, and the
surrounding countryside. We will find ourselves in small brick churches with
plain sanctuaries and scuffed linoleum floors, in Gothic cathedrals where

light filters through stained glass windows, and in theater-like auditoriums boasting state-of-the-art electronics. The sermons we hear will be equally diverse. Differences in sermon content, form, and rhetorical style will reveal contrasting theological visions, hermeneutical commitments, and cultures of reception.

In many of the largest and youngest Protestant congregations, we are likely to hear (and see!) sermons whose approach to Scripture and theology signal affinity with evangelical and Pentecostal traditions. These sermons often feature an informal style and significant technological support.[1] Sermons in these settings may take the shape of verse-by-verse exposition, a series of mini-talks punctuated by video and music, or extended teaching about doctrine in a well-illustrated thirty-minute presentation.

Much evangelical preaching rests on the hermeneutical assumption that the meaning of a biblical text is univocal (singular) and relatively fixed. The preacher's task is to unlock this meaning by working out the grammar and vocabulary of the text. While there is room for engaging stories or inductive exploration of an idea, these strategies are meant to amplify a stable, clearly stated truth about God and the human condition, often "applied" to the lives of listeners in a move that seeks to evoke intellectual assent, emotional commitment, and behavioral response.

Evangelical and Pentecostal preaching and worship styles are mixing in North America today to such an extent that they are not always easily distinguished. Features of worship once more or less exclusive to Pentecostal churches—raising of hands in prayer and praise, "singing in the Spirit," and offering public prayers for healing, for example—are frequently practiced in independent evangelical megachurches. Conversely, Pentecostal preachers have picked up subject matter not native to their traditions—particularly "health-and-wealth" preaching—so much so that some Pentecostal scholars worry that the distinctive strengths of Pentecostal preaching and witness are being left behind.[2] The Azusa Street Revival of 1906 in Los Angeles, California, to which many American Pentecostal denominations trace their roots, centered on the outpouring and vibrant manifestation of the Holy Spirit. This outpouring, in addition to producing ecstatic speech and an emphasis on "baptism in the Spirit," was countercultural, multiethnic, racially mixed, and led from the pulpit by both women and men.[3] Eric Patterson and Edmund Rybarczyk worry that traditional Pentecostal themes, including "prophetic critiques of culture," are being traded in for therapeutic, success-oriented preaching.[4] Cheryl Bridges Johns finds that Pentecostal preaching at its best continues to occur in urban contexts amid cultures of "otherness" outside the purview of the mainstream, as it did at its beginnings.[5] Johns expresses concern that prosperous Pentecostal preachers and their congregations readily forget that manifestations of the Spirit's power have led to deep social change.[6] If Pentecostal preaching can reconnect its emphasis on the in-breaking power of the Spirit with its countercultural, socially reconstructive legacy, it may prove to be a crucial mainspring for healing deep divides in North American Christianity and culture.

Another homiletical tradition we would encounter on our tour would be represented in churches of the North American Protestant "mainline" traditions, including Presbyterian, Methodist, Lutheran, Episcopal, Disciples of Christ, United Church of Christ, and Reformed Church in America congregations. This is where we are most likely to hear sermons influenced by "the New Homiletic," a powerful body of homiletical theory and theology that gained momentum in the 1970s and has shaped the homiletical work of several generations of preachers.

Hermeneutically, the New Homiletic tends to see the Bible less as a repository of fixed ideas than as a revealing lens, either theological or literary, that enables fresh perception of divine redemptive activity in the world. In this tradition, the sermon becomes an event of discovery that leads to a transformed vision of God, self, and world. Evangelical scholars and preachers cautiously embrace certain New Homiletical insights. They may bring listeners' experience into dialogue with a biblical text, preach with more attentiveness to the function of a particular biblical genre (psalm of lament, parable, or proverb, for example), or develop a sermon's ideas inductively rather than deductively. However, some evangelical scholars contend that shifting authority away from the biblical text itself to the experiential event of preaching "raises serious questions about the nature of inspiration and biblical revelation."[7]

Also prominently represented on our preaching tour would be the homiletical tradition that is arguably North America's most distinctive contribution to homiletics worldwide, African American preaching. Practiced in the pulpits of historically black denominational congregations as well as black or multiethnic congregations in other traditions, African American preaching in different contexts may share features with each of the other homiletic traditions discussed so far. Yet African American preaching retains some distinctive theological perspectives, hermeneutical emphases, subject matters, and rhetorical styles. This uniqueness derives from its origins in the social, economic, political, and religious history and legacy of chattel slavery in the United States. African American preachers declare God's redemptive acts from within, and for the sake of, the distinct social reality of being black in America. As a consequence, preachers who do not live this reality themselves cannot simply appropriate the African American preaching tradition for themselves and their settings with integrity. Nonetheless, preachers of other traditions can learn from African American preaching on many levels. More will be said of this later in this chapter.

The homily in the Roman Catholic mass is yet another distinctive preaching form on the North American homiletical landscape. Perhaps no preaching tradition has undergone such rapid, worldwide, and theologically conscientious revision in recent years as the Roman Catholic homily. While Vatican II restored the homily to the weekly mass, it was not until the 1982 publication *Fulfilled in Your Hearing* (a detailed discussion of guidelines for Catholic preaching produced by the National Committee of Catholic Bishops) that the theological and theoretical criteria for a restored preaching practice were fully articulated.[8] At first, results in local parishes were mixed. Priests were charged to engage biblical texts with imaginative alertness to their cultural relevance yet were struggling at the same time to overcome a long tradition of priestly aloofness from the culture of the pews.[9] Some local priests had few, if any, role models for a distinctive Roman Catholic approach to preaching.

Today, however, a distinctive Catholic preaching tradition shaped by a deep liturgical sensibility is beginning to flourish. At its best, Catholic preaching holds Word, altar, and world closely together. Characteristically, the homily aligns lectionary texts with the symbolic world of the liturgy and, from that perspective, "names grace" in the everyday world.[10] Preaching not "on" the text but *through* text and liturgy into the world, Catholic preaching is acutely attuned to the connections between liturgy and life, sacrament and social justice.[11] Insights drawn from the New Homiletic as well as postmodern approaches are being transplanted into the sacramentally rich and liturgically deep soil of Roman Catholic worship.[12]

Finally, the future of North American preaching is being shaped by the preaching emerging in worshipping communities that claim a "hyphenated" identity—Korean-American, Arab-American, Ghanaian-American, Mexican-American, and more. These preaching traditions reflect influences from Central America, Africa, East Asia, the Middle East, and elsewhere, often emphasizing preservation of preaching in the native language of the first generation, even when English-language preaching is also offered.

Clearly, across this diverse preaching landscape, one preacher's sign of hope will raise concerns for another. Some evangelicals share the concerns cited above about New Homiletical approaches. Conversely, preachers in the New Homiletic tradition worry about any hermeneutic that confines the grammar of God's living Word today to that of ancient Scripture. African American preachers worry about preaching that leaves congregations intellectually informed but unmoved in body and spirit. And, as we have seen, Pentecostal scholars hope to see preachers in their tradition reclaim a critical stance toward dominant cultural norms. There are reasons for concern about the future of North American preaching but ample reasons for hope as well.

Scanning for Signs of Hope

On this map I locate myself as a critically appreciative member of the New Homiletic neighborhood. I recognize certain blind spots in New Homiletic approaches to preaching. Some of them have been proposed by some of the original architects of New Homiletical theory. Five of the scholars to whom the New Homiletical turn is credited gathered in 2007, along with other homiletics scholars, to review their original theories and consider possible emendations. One crucial recognition was that we can no longer treat human experience as a universal matter, as many of the early theories did. The trouble with assuming human universals, noted Ruthanna B. Hooke, "is that such 'universal' experience is often the experience of the dominant class—white, heterosexual, middle class, and male."[13] Both biblical interpretation and the overt claims of our preaching need to take into account the difference social location and culture make.

To this I would add that we must pay more attention to the play of power in every preaching event. Michel Foucault's observation that every discourse manifests power needs to be inscribed on a Post-it and tacked to our computer screens and pulpits.[14] There are hidden histories of privilege in the texts we interpret and the interpreters whose voices we privilege. The authority of the pulpit carries the power to influence listeners' thinking and practice. To imagine it is only "the truth of Scripture" or "the power of the Spirit" that accounts for the influence of preaching is naive at best, disingenuous at worst. Gifted preachers in particular—the ones everyone wants to hear—bear special responsibility to use the pulpit to amplify those voices in and beyond the church to which few listen.

Another product of the 2007 conference was more a question than a pronouncement: Had New Homiletic theories too hastily thrown out the propositional baby with the authoritarian pulpit bathwater? In other words, had New Homiletic theory steered away too sharply from sermons that clarify doctrine and teach critical thinking about Christian faith? Many in the pews today are unfamiliar with Christianity's basic narratives or creeds. Sermons that teach are back on the preaching menu.

Noting these revisions, I still share in the New Homileticians' affirmation that the preaching event discloses what God has done, is doing, and promises yet to do in gathering all things into the redeemed, and redeeming, future of the risen Jesus Christ, firstborn of God's new creation. Certainly not all in the New Homiletical neighborhood would embrace this claim, or at least this way of expressing it. But I take it as one of the movement's central contributions.[15]

As a preacher and teacher of preaching who owns these homiletical and theological convictions, I find three developments on the homiletical scene today intriguing. First, I am struck by the creative ways that both my students and the working preachers I know are engaging the Internet, not simply as a ready source of material, but as a learning environment. Second, students and working preachers are turning with fresh interest to African American homiletical practice and theory as a resource for grappling with the new challenges of a national scene that is filled with cultural diversities and tensions, marked by an ever-increasing gap between rich and poor, and faced with deeply racialized issues of justice. Third, both preachers and scholars have taken notice of developments around three particular genres within postmodern popular rhetoric that have remarkable affinities with genres of biblical rhetoric and, in turn, seem to suggest new departures for preaching. These three are: (a) the TED talk; (b) ironic modes of speech in everyday conversation and in entertainment; and (c) parabolic and apocalyptic narratives in literature, films, and television series designed for teenage and adult consumers. In the next section, I explore each of these developments and point to some of the ways they are shaping preaching today.

Promising Signs on the Homiletical Landscape

1. Preachers are turning to the Internet, not only as a ready source of useful material, but as a learning environment.

Internet resources for preachers abound. At our fingertips are thousands of sermons in print, audio, and video formats as well as multiple websites devoted to preaching and its component tasks of biblical and cultural interpretation. The Internet has also begun to function in still another way: preachers are making strategic use of the Internet as a resource for critical reflection on their own and others' preaching and as a platform where communities of like-minded preachers can support and challenge one another.

It used to be that preachers were rarely exposed to the preaching of others except in print form. They tended to work, after all, in parallel—on Saturday nights or Sunday mornings. Today, thanks to the Internet, a world of preaching in worship contexts and traditions similar to and different from one's own is a few clicks away.

Apart from preaching itself, nothing trains our ears and creative instincts for preaching like listening to one another preach. Whether we agree with what we're hearing or not is not the point; we learn in any case. Furthermore, the Internet allows us to create communities of learning among preachers. Together, they can listen to sermons on the web and share their reactions. They can share the challenges of parish and nonparish ministry, trade insights, and discuss what they're reading. They can view one another's sermons and get informed feedback.

Research shows that preachers who are part of a committed group of colleagues that works out a specific plan for expanding their knowledge of preaching together and exchanges supportive and knowledgeable feedback reap at least three rewards: (1) their preaching improves measurably; (2) their satisfaction in ministry improves measurably; and (3) their congregations express greater satisfaction with the preaching they are hearing.[16]

Growing interest among preachers of all traditions in working together to improve their preaching is a promising sign for the future of North American preaching. And the Internet is opening up new strategies for such collaboration.

2. The riches of African American preaching traditions are being studied with new vigor by preachers not only within these traditions but also beyond them. Preachers are accessing sermons in print and via the Internet, as well as reading publications by African American scholars in biblical studies, theological studies, homiletics, and cultural studies.

There has always been interest in African American preaching among preachers both within and beyond black traditions. Perhaps no rhetorician of the twentieth century has been so thoroughly studied by scholars both black and white as Martin Luther King Jr. However, apart from a few particularly prominent figures—Gardner Taylor, Samuel Proctor, Prathia Hall, and a handful of others—much of the week-to-week preaching of African American preachers was largely unfamiliar to white scholars and preachers. Black women preachers were all but invisible until recent efforts by black academics began to bring their sermons and homiletical methods into view.[17]

Today students and working preachers alike are eager to learn from and about black preaching. Yet, as indicated earlier in this chapter, preachers outside African American preaching traditions need to be acutely aware that while they can respectfully learn from the sociopolitical dynamics of the black church and from its preachers, to imagine that non-blacks can "appropriate" or inhabit this tradition without regard to the particularities of its social location is both disingenuous and misguided.

That said, preachers of all traditions in North America need to *attend to* black preaching traditions. They need, first, to understand the critical role black preaching has played, and continues to play, in sustaining African American survival. Amid the adversities of chattel slavery, Jim Crow laws, and contemporary situations fraught with deadly racist violence, black preaching has fostered a strong identity for blacks, mobilized not only the black church but churches of many traditions, and called society as a whole to account. Understanding this history is critical for preachers who must address a North American society becoming evermore divided ethnically and economically, one in which racist assumptions continue to persist beneath the surface of economic and social debates.

Aiding preachers' quest to learn what African American homiletics can teach them is a growing body of scholarship produced by black homileticians, biblical scholars, and sociologists. This work not only helps preachers within black preaching traditions grasp the historical, rhetorical, theological, and cultural roots of their own tradition but introduces the internal structure of this homiletical tradition to those outside it.[18]

Key features of African American preaching were first systematized and brought to the attention of the scholarly academy by such pioneering African American homileticians as Henry H. Mitchell, Gardner C. Taylor, Samuel D. Proctor, James Earl Massey, and James Henry Harris.[19] The work of a generation following closely on their heels deepened specific dimensions of the practice and context of African American preaching. Cleophus J. LaRue's work on African American hermeneutics, Teresa Fry Brown's writing on the body and voice in proclamation, Melva Wilson Costen's publications on African American worship, and Frank Thomas's work on celebration in African American preaching all contributed to a multidimensional understanding of preaching in black traditions.[20] A rising generation of younger scholars including Luke A. Powery, Kenyatta R. Gilbert, and Debra J. Mumford continues to develop a more fine-grained sense of African American preaching historically, theologically, and in relation to African American musical cultures.

Preachers have been enriched as well by the work of New Testament scholars like Brian Blount, who, as a preacher himself, is consistently attentive to the homiletical implications of the texts he is engaging (most notably, Mark and Revelation).[21] Widening the theo-rhetorical lens, sociologist Ralph Basui Watkins evaluates hip-hop theologically as well as culturally, revealing the theological roots of its prophetic impulses.[22] Works such as Richard Lischer's study of the world-making rhetoric of Martin Luther King Jr. and Jared Alcantara's recent study of improvisation in the transcultural preaching of Gardner Taylor provide examples of homiletical work strengthened and informed by attention to black preaching.[23]

The interaction of preaching traditions is not merely an academic exercise. It is a lived event in college, seminary, and divinity school classrooms where student bodies are increasingly diverse. In these environments, different preaching traditions can sharpen one another, as iron sharpens iron.

3. Both preachers and scholars are exploring remarkable parallels between rhetorical forms prominent in postmodern popular culture today and rhetorical forms in the biblical tradition. Particularly intriguing in this regard are: (a) the popularity of the Internet phenomenon known as the "TED talk"; (b) the pervasiveness of irony in postmodern attitudes and conversation; and (c) the proliferation of novels, films, and television series in the genre of parabolic/apocalyptic narrative. Each has its counterpart in biblical literature.

a) TED Talks and the Teaching Sermon: Proposal and Demonstration

Although preachers influenced by the New Homiletic have, for the most part, been mistrustful of sermons that begin with a proposition and then demonstrate it, the sheer popularity of the web phenomenon known as the TED talk suggests it may be time to reconsider this prejudice. The popularity of the TED talk suggests that it is possible to propose without being authoritarian.[24] In a TED talk, one person, generally an expert in his or her field, speaks from a stage casually and often without notes, proposing an idea or way of approaching a problem, backing it up with arguments and data, and spelling out the difference it makes for our thinking or behavior.

TED, as the website states, "is a nonprofit devoted to spreading ideas, usually in the form of short, powerful talks (18 minutes or less). TED began in 1984 as a conference where Technology, Entertainment, and Design converged, and today covers almost all topics—from science to business to global issues—in more than 100 languages."[25] Widely shared and discussed on social media, TED talks deal with all kinds of questions an information-hungry public is buzzing about. The TED staff selects speakers with care and filters the talks, posting only the best of them online.

Most TED talks are more deductive than inductive in design. Their most typical form could be described as proposal-and-demonstration. Blogging on *Second Nature*, which describes itself as "an online journal for critical thinking about technology and new media in light of the Christian tradition," Michael Toy comments that TED talks "have evolved into a cultural phenomenon that begs for comparison with our traditional sermon."[26] TED talks are crisp and rhetorically persuasive, notes Toy: "Using scientific data or qualitative research, presenters pack an informative, persuasive, and usually rhetorically excellent message into an aurally and visually stimulating package that is shorter than twenty minutes." Even their rhetorical purpose is sermon-like: these talks offer reliable scientific or social-scientific data, "explain what it means, and then explain to the audience how to live a more fulfilling life in light of this new data."[27] Preachers should take note, says Toy: "It seems that motivating people to live a good and fulfilling life— once a distinctly Christian endeavor—has passed into the realm of the secular world." Furthermore, like sermons, TED talks "do indeed aim at creating in the listeners a reframing of belief" and even "involve love of neighbor (often through love of self or self-care)."[28]

Grammatically speaking, the proposals that TED talks support are stated as propositions. Their immense popularity with a postmodern web culture suggests that propositions, as such, are not the communicational problem for contemporary listeners, whether in the pew or anywhere else, that New Homileticians sometimes suppose them to be. The problem occurs when propositions function like hammers instead of keys that can open doors. Hammer-like propositions, instead of offering proposals for listeners to consider and demonstrating why they are worthy of assent, *demand* submission on the basis of the speaker's personal authority or the authority of source that cannot be questioned. Keys, on the other hand, are entrusted to the listener. They can become valuable tools that listeners use to explore their world.

There are numerous biblical texts that take this form. John 10 contains what amount to three short "sermons" that begin with a proposal and then proceed to demonstration. Sentences in propositional form begin each homily: "Anyone who does not enter the sheepfold by the gate but climbs in by another way is a thief and a bandit. The one who enters by the gate is the shepherd" (John 10:1–2), "I am the gate for the sheep" (John 10:7), and "I am the good shepherd" (10:11). Each proposal is demonstrated with further observations, all working with the extended metaphor of sheep herding.

Other examples are the teaching discourses on wisdom in Proverbs 7 and 8. After beginning, "My child, keep my words and store up my commandments with you" (Prov. 7:1), the teacher introduces Wisdom figured as a trustworthy sister (7:4). After contrasting Wisdom with the wiles of a prostitute in chapter 7 and celebrating Wisdom as a wise teacher in chapter 8, the discourse ends propositionally, as well: "For whoever finds me finds life" (8:35).

African American preaching includes many sermons that follow a proposal-and-demonstration pattern and do so with compelling elegance. The well-known sermon by Martin Luther King Jr., "A Knock at Midnight," demonstrates the power of this sermon design in the hands of an expert crafter of language. Three propositions anchor King's opening move: "It is midnight in the social order"; "It is midnight in the psychological order"; and "It is also midnight within the moral order." Each is developed by appeal to the common experience of King's listeners. These sentences take propositional form, yet rhetorically, they do not function as authoritarian claims but as proposals. One reason for this is that they make their proposals metaphorically, suggesting a new way of seeing reality. The sermon that unfolds leaves listeners attentive in the midnight of social change, whether they are those who knock on the doors of justice or reach to open the lock and wait for the dawn of a new day.

Another example of proposal-and-demonstration preaching is Claudette Anderson Copeland's sermon, "Tamar's Torn Robe." Two propositions set the sermon in motion: "Christian life calls us to make decisions. But life sometime has already *made some* decisions for us." To back up these claims, Copeland does deft teaching to demonstrate how various systems—family legacies, patriarchy, confusion, and the silencing of women—contribute to the challenges urban black women face. Weaving in and out of the story of Tamar in 2 Samuel 13, Copeland encourages women to use their voices as Tamar did to seek health, divine help, and change.[29]

As these examples suggest, some intriguing convergences are emerging between the proposal-and-demonstration rhetoric of TED talks and contemporary preaching.

b) Irony in Postmodern Rhetoric, Scripture, and Preaching

Irony, particularly tropes of ironic literalism, are a staple ingredient in contemporary conversation and culture. Irony plays with literalism, sometimes to expose disturbing social realities.

Irony is not, of course, an innovation of contemporary popular culture, although in recent years it has become much more the norm than the edgy exception. In the late 1970s, the television show *Saturday Night Live* featured actress Gilda Radner playing an elderly, somewhat-hard-of-hearing literalist by the name of Emily Litella. When the persecution of Jews in the Soviet Union was being discussed in the news but still ignored by many people, the show featured Radner's Miss Litella pursuing a persistent monologue wanting to know why everyone was so worked up about "Soviet jewelry."[30] Her rant worked ironically to expose the absurd indifference of most of the public to the Soviet oppression of Jews.

Ironic literalism is also a favored trope of stand-up comic and talk-show host Ellen DeGeneres. Pretending naïve curiosity, she raises questions and pursues possible answers, unmasking the pretense of those of us who refuse to admit the depth of our prejudices or the banality of our self-obsessions. Her talent for ironic social critique came through when she (ironically!) hosted the 2006 Oscars Film Awards ceremony, despite being shunned by many for making public her lesbian identity. DeGeneres quipped,

> What a wonderful night, such diversity in the room, in a year when there's [sic] been so many negative things said about people's race, religion, and sexual orientation. And I want to put this out there: If there weren't blacks, Jews and gays, there would be no Oscars, or anyone named Oscar, when you think about that.[31]

Biblical texts, too, make use of irony. Isaiah 44 contains a clearly ironic tale of an idol-maker's use of a tree:

> He cuts down cedars or chooses a holm tree or an oak and lets it grow strong among the trees of the forest. He plants a cedar and the rain nourishes it. Then it can be used as fuel. Part of it he takes and warms himself; he kindles a fire and bakes bread. Then he makes a god and worships it, makes it a carved image and bows down before it. Half of it he burns in the fire; over this half he roasts meat, eats it and is satisfied. He also warms himself and says, "Ah, I am warm, I can feel the fire!" The rest of it he makes into a god, his idol, bows down to it and worships it; he prays to it and says, "Save me, for you are my god!" (Isa. 44:14–17)

In their study of folly, parody, and irony in Scripture and preaching, Charles L. Campbell and Johann H. Cilliers underscore the irony of Jesus' crucifixion. Roman crucifixion was meant to be a humiliating and deadly parody of kingly enthronement. Ironically, those who robed Jesus in purple, pressed a crown of thorns on his head, and taunted him to act with kingly authority to free himself from the cross were telling more truth than they knew.[32]

Irony is a well-established feature of African American preaching, deriving from the trope of "signifying" in which a black individual appears to speak innocently while delivering an incisive critique of the behavior of members of dominant culture (typically whites) in an immediate situation.

Handled poorly, of course, irony easily degenerates into raw sarcasm; but handled well, it can be highly effective for contemporary listeners across the cultural, ethnic, and denominational spectrum. Many leading preachers of the early twenty-first century have taken a cue from the late Fred B. Craddock, whose deft use of irony remains exemplary. In a sermon based on Hebrews 12:1–13, Craddock develops a sense of what "looking to Jesus" *does* mean by portraying what it does *not* mean.

> It happened in Georgia. A man was executed. The warden came out and said exactly seven minutes after midnight this person was pronounced dead by the coroner. Outside ringing the prison in that late-night hour were people holding up Bible verses and the name of Jesus. And when the warden said he had been executed, they applauded and praised Jesus. A human life. . . . The bumper sticker in front of me on an old truck said, "I love my wife, and I love Jesus. The rest of you can go to hell."[33]

Lillian Daniel, a pastor in the Chicago area, offers another important example of irony in contemporary preaching. She begins a sermon based on Matthew 6:19–34 with an ironic interrogation of North American's fascination with evermore, and evermore expensive, things—things whose overabundance calls for ever-larger storage facilities. Playing on the element of the absurd in irony, Daniels muses on a news story about the conversion of an urban high-rise apartment building into "luxury storage facilities." Daniels wonders aloud whether the unit is appointed with lavender-scented mothballs, cleaned once a week by uniformed staff, and—as predicted by Jesus— invaded by moths and vermin. Then such luxury storage would be reserved for highly educated insects and rodents.[34] Other contemporary preachers who make deft use of irony include Barbara Brown Taylor, Anna Carter Florence, Brian K. Blount, and M. Craig Barnes.[35]

c) Apocalyptic Parables of Good and Evil in Popular Culture and Scripture

A third rhetorical form embraced by contemporary popular culture is the extended, apocalyptic parable. *The Hunger Games*, a popular series of books and films, and *The Walking Dead*, a hit comic book series and television show, are just two examples of a genre that has been well-represented across many media in the last twenty years.

The Hunger Games and its sequels, written by Suzanne Collins, portray a grim post-apocalyptic reality in which a centralized authority selects two young people, a boy and a girl (called "tributes"), from each of twelve districts to compete in a ritual contest of strength, combat, and survival in which death is almost inevitable. One alone survives through a combination of skill, luck, and selective loyalty. *The Walking Dead*, based on a comic book series and a long-running cable television series, focuses on a group of survivors of worldwide warfare in a devastated Georgia landscape. Among the horrors of this grim reality are "walkers"—zombies, the "living dead," some of whom are actually related to the company of survivors. Being bitten by walkers is a constant danger; the bite transmits the infection that dooms those wounded to be reanimated as walkers themselves.

What is striking about these extended apocalyptic narratives is that each of them examines the dark side of ambitions and forms of entertainment that contemporary society actually values. *The Hunger Games* are, in a sense, a dark version of the survival shows that have taken television audiences by storm since tests of endurance like *Survivor* and *The Amazing Race* first aired in 2000 and 2001, respectively.

In the dark, apocalyptic world of *The Hunger Games*, to survive is a dubious victory; one who lives is doomed to compete again. Victories, such as they are, come in the form of small moral triumphs of loyalty or courage but grant no real leverage against the system. Sport has become an instrument of control. *The Walking Dead* confronts a society bent on staving off aging as much as possible, as long as possible, with the nightmarish possibility that becoming victims of our own success might come to pass after nothing more than a slight, unfortunate genetic mutation. The worlds these shows create take seriously the power of evil to distort even the best of human aspirations, with horrifying results.

The biblical genre of apocalypse, like the fantasy apocalyptic worlds of novel, film, and television, takes seriously the life-devouring nature of evil. The cosmic dislocations of Mark's "little apocalypse" (chapter 13) and the beasts of John's apocalyptic vision in Revelation have their counterparts in postmodern reimaginations of the future.

It is likely a weakness of contemporary preaching that it simply does not take the human capacity for evil seriously enough or persuade Christians that there is anything worth fighting for. When we preach in ways that comfort our listeners with the idea that Jesus' work on the cross excuses them from all conflict, we sell the gospel short and fail to speak to a world where new, deadly conflicts arise almost weekly and seem only to fester, never to end. Tapping the biblical genre of apocalypse may have much to say to present-day congregations.

New Testament scholar Brian Blount's 2011 Beecher Lectures examine the parallels between extended apocalyptic parables, ancient and contemporary. With his characteristic preacher's eye, Blount suggests ways we might take up the apocalyptic in our preaching that not only connect with postmodern imagination but introduce genuine hope for a different future brought about by the God who overcomes death in all its forms.

From Signs of Hope to Speaking Hope

Without doubt there are many signs of hope for the future of preaching in North America. Scanning the landscape with my revised, renewed-homiletic lenses, I have identified just three. They count for me as signs of hope because they signify that preachers are seriously engaged in the business of discerning how to speak gospel in a language that twenty-first-century listeners recognize as their own tongue.

Michael Toy, whose insights we considered in connection with the TED talk phenomenon, makes this wise observation: "It is up to the church to find what is distinct, specific to the church, and unique to Christianity not just in theological belief, but also in transformative effect."[36]

What is distinct and transformative in Christian belief and preaching is our testimony to the God who has already inaugurated future hope in the resurrection life of Jesus. Savvy speakers can generate optimism, but what is at stake in Christian preaching is something more. The issue is not simply whether we can learn to speak "in the native language of each" (Acts 2:6) but how to proclaim divinely inaugurated hope to a generation that distrusts hope itself.

Maybe this crisis of hope is one reason why a new generation of preachers of all ethnicities and theological traditions is so eager to learn from African American preaching. Nooses and police dogs, bullets and boots have not been able to silence the shout or the song of the black church in North America. African American preaching and worship is a celebration of God-generated, evil-destroying, world-renewing hope on the basis of a testimony it has never ceased to trust: *Our Risen Lord bears the marks of crucifixion.* Perhaps if it is hope we are looking for, these are the truest signs of all.

What Shall We Say?

THOMAS LYNCH

A triptych for Thomas G. Long:

teacher, preacher, presbyter

I.

The etymology is perilous:
pulpit from *pulpitum*, meaning *scaffold*,
by which we come, at length, to *catafalque*—
those f's and a's, like tongue-and-groove boards,
like rope enough to hang, or hoist, or let
a corpse down to its permanent repose.
One platform's raised; one frames a coffin's rest.
So, first the elocution, then the wake?
Like lamentations or the case of Job—
that vexing, god-awful, comfortless book.
And yet we rise to the occasion,
Sunday after Sunday after Sunday.
A bit of Scripture, a psalm or poem,
something that happened in the week just past;
we try to weave them all together as
if to say a loving God's in charge.
As if we were certain of a loving God.
We see by faith. We live in hope. We love.
Or play the odds, as Pascal did. We fall.
Sometimes it all seems quite impossible.
And yet we rise again and walk the plank,
and sing into oblivion good news:
Unto God the glory, all praise, all thanks!
while nodding congregants loll in their pews.

II.

Imagine Tom out on the fire escape,
between the world at large and inner life,
edging the proscenium, downstage right,
whilst curios and characters and shades

unveil themselves as dancing beauties do.
I have tricks in my pocket, things up my sleeve!
Upstage, sheer curtains rise, transparencies:
Truth in the pleasant guise of illusion.

Like John on Patmos, John the Harbinger—
voices crying out of the wilderness—
Make straight ye the Lord's way! quoth Isaiah.
Eschatology and Apocalypse:

Think Esmeralda in the cathedral,
Jim Hawkins in the rigging, chased by Hands
or Ishmael, just flotsam at the end,
alone, before God and all these people.

Or Montaigne in his tower library:
The whole of Man's estate in every man.
Or Yeats pacing the boards at Ballylee:
"How can we know the dancer from the dance?"

Thus, exegetes and preachers on their own
hold forth, against a never-ceasing din
of second-guessing, out there on their limbs:
Have faith! Behold, the mystery! Behold!

III.

That fresco of the Sermon on the Mount
by Fra Angelico (dear brother John)
shows Jesus semicircled by his men,
gilt-haloed Galileans, but for one,
who will betray him later with a kiss,
atop their sandstone tuffets, rapt, engaged.
He's going on about beatitudes,
fulfillments of the law, the words to pray.
Outside the frame, unseen, a multitude
leans in to listen to the hermeneutics,
which are not without some challenges, to wit:
though we be smitten, turn the other cheek,
go the second mile, love our enemies;
while we're forgiven only so much as
we forgive those who trespass against us.
A certain eye-for-eyeness to that scheme,
a tooth-for-toothedness. A quid pro quo?
As if, to finally get, we must let go?
Sometimes it's so, sometimes it isn't? So,
what shall we say to these things? Who's to know?
Say who abides in love abides in God.
Say God is love. Love God. Love one another.
Say grace is undeserved and plentiful.
Say if we're saved, it's mostly from ourselves.

Contributors

Sally A. Brown, Elizabeth M. Engle Associate Professor of Preaching and Worship, Princeton Theological Seminary

Teresa Fry Brown, Bandy Professor of Preaching, Candler School of Theology, Emory University

Craig Dykstra, Research Professor of Practical Theology, Duke Divinity School, Duke University

Anna Carter Florence, Peter Marshall Professor of Preaching, Columbia Theological Seminary

Scott Black Johnston, Senior Pastor, Fifth Avenue Presbyterian Church (New York, New York)

Jin S. Kim, Pastor, Church of All Nations, Minneapolis, Minnesota, and founder of Underground Seminary

Jacqueline J. Lewis, Pastor, Middle Collegiate Church, New York City, and Executive Director of The Middle Project, New York

Richard Lischer, James T. and Alice Mead Cleland Professor of Preaching, Duke Divinity School, Duke University

Thomas Lynch, poet and author

John S. McClure, Charles G. Finney Professor of Preaching and Worship, Vanderbilt Divinity School, Vanderbilt University

Alyce M. McKenzie, Le Van Professor of Preaching and Worship, Perkins School of Theology, Southern Methodist University

Gail R. O'Day, Dean and Professor of New Testament and Preaching, Wake Forest University School of Divinity, Wake Forest University

Gabriel Salguero, Pastor, The Lamb's Church, New York City, and President of the National Latino Evangelical Coalition (*editor's note:* He is now serving as pastor of Iglesia El Calvario, a multiethnic church in Orlando, Florida)

Ted A. Smith, Associate Professor of Preaching and Ethics, Candler School of Theology, Emory University

Nibs Stroupe, Pastor, Oakhurst Presbyterian Church, Decatur, Georgia

Barbara Brown Taylor, Butman Professor of Religion & Philosophy, Piedmont College

Leonora Tubbs Tisdale, Clement-Muehl Professor of Homiletics, Yale Divinity School, Yale University

Notes

FOREWORD

1. Thomas G. Long, *Shepherds and Bathrobes: Sermons for Advent, Christmas, and Epiphany* (Lima, OH: CSS Publishing Co., 1987), 7.

2. John Calvin, *Institutes of the Christian Religion*, 1.1.1; ed. John T. McNeill, trans. Ford Lewis Battles, LCC (Philadelphia: Westminster Press, 1960), 1:35.

3. Thomas G. Long, *The Witness of Preaching*, 3rd ed. (Louisville, KY: Westminster John Knox Press, 2016), 2–3, emphasis added.

4. Thomas G. Long, *Accompany Them with Singing: The Christian Funeral* (Louisville, KY: Westminster John Knox, 2009), 9.

5. Thomas G. Long, *Preaching from Memory to Hope* (Louisville, KY: Westminster John Knox Press, 2009), xiii.

6. Craig Dykstra, "Pastoral and Ecclesial Imagination," in *For Life Abundant: Practical Theology, Theological Education, and Christian Ministry*, ed. Dorothy C. Bass and Craig Dykstra (Grand Rapids: Eerdmans, 2008), 41.

INTRODUCTION

1. Thomas G. Long, *The Witness of Preaching*, 3rd ed. (Louisville, KY: Westminster John Knox Press, 2016), x.

CHAPTER 1. SHAPED BY HEARING

1. Unless otherwise indicated, Scripture quotations in this chapter are the author's own translation.

2. Two of Fred B. Craddock's most significant works, *As One without Authority* (Nashville: Abingdon, 1971) and *Overhearing the Gospel* (Nashville: Abingdon, 1978), acutely name the tensive relationship between pastoral authority and proclamation. Even though these books were written in the 1970s, the dilemma they name remains poignant forty years later.

3. See James Carleton Paget and Joachim Schaper, eds., *The New Cambridge History of the Bible* (Cambridge: Cambridge University Press, 2013).

4. See Derek A. Olsen, *Reading Matthew with Monks: Liturgical Interpretation in Anglo-Saxon England* (Collegeville, MN: Liturgical Press, 2015).

5. Rowan Williams, *Being Christian: Baptism, Bible, Eucharist, Prayer* (Grand Rapids: Eerdmans, 2014), 21–22.

6. Joseph Sittler, *Gravity and Grace: Reflections and Provocations* (Minneapolis: Augsburg Fortress, 1986), 50–51.

7. For a fuller discussion of this aspect of preaching, see Gail R. O'Day, "Bible and Sermon: The Conversation between Text and Preacher," in Barry L. Callen, ed., *Sharing Heaven's Music: Essays in Honor of James Earl Massey* (Nashville: Abingdon, 1995), 69–81.

8. "No News Is Bad News" is the title of chapter 2 of Thomas G. Long, *Preaching from Memory to Hope* (Louisville, KY: Westminster John Knox, 2009).

CHAPTER 2. FORM FOLLOWS FUNCTION

1. Thomas G. Long, *Preaching and the Literary Forms of the Bible* (Louisville, KY: Westminster John Knox Press, 1989), 13–14.

2. Thomas G. Long, "And How Shall They Hear? The Listener in Contemporary Preaching," in *Listening to the Word: Studies in Honor of Fred B. Craddock*, ed. Gail R. O'Day and Thomas G. Long (Nashville: Abingdon Press, 1993).

3. Thomas G. Long, *Testimony: Talking Ourselves into Being Christian* (San Francisco: Jossey-Bass, 2004), 4.

4. Thomas G. Long, *The Witness of Preaching*, 3rd ed. (Louisville, KY: Westminster John Knox Press, 2016), 136.

5. Ibid., 137.

6. Ibid., 136. See also Halford Luccock, *In the Minister's Workshop* (New York: Abingdon Cokesbury, 1944), 118.

7. Ken Unterer, *Preaching Better: Practical Suggestions for Homilists* (Mahwah, NJ: Paulist Press, 1999), 30.

8. Long, *Preaching and the Literary Forms of the Bible*, 24.

9. Alyce M. McKenzie, *Preaching Proverbs: Wisdom for the Pulpit* (Louisville, KY: Westminster John Knox Press, 1996).

10. Stephen Crites, "The Narrative Quality of Experience," *Journal of the American Academy of Religion* 23, no. 3 (September 1971): 291–311.

11. Thomas G. Long, "Out of the Loop: The Changing Practice of Preaching," in *What's the Shape of Narrative Preaching? Essays in Honor of Eugene L. Lowry*, ed. Mike Graves and David J. Schlafer (St. Louis: Chalice Press, 2008), 126.

12. Ibid., 129.

13. Long, *Preaching and the Literary Forms of the Bible*, 72, 74.

14. Ibid., 100.

15. Long, "Out of the Loop," 129–30.

CHAPTER 3. CRAFTING A SERMON SERIES

1. The RCL was developed by an ecumenical council, The Consultation on Common Texts (CCT). The CCT's introductory article, "The Revised Common Lectionary" (1992), remains one of the most helpful explanations of the theological logic of the RCL. It can be found on their website, commontexts.org, at http://www.commontexts.org/wp-content/uploads/2015/11/RCL_Introduction_Web.pdf.

2. "Using the Revised Common Lectionary," section IV in *The Revised Common Lectionary: Consultation on Common Texts*, http://www.commontexts.org/wp-content/uploads/2015/11/RCL_Introduction_Web.pdf: "The Old Testament passage is perceived as a parallel, a contrast, or as a type leading to its fulfillment in the gospel."

3. Thomas G. Long, *The Witness of Preaching*, 3rd ed. (Louisville, KY: Westminster John Knox Press, 2016), 82.

4. Ibid., 83.

5. Timothy Matthew Slemmons, *Year D: A Quadrennial Supplement to the Revised Common Lectionary* (Eugene, OR: Wipf & Stock Publishers, 2012). Others have assembled *lectio continua* alternatives to the RCL, a wonderful example of which is Luther Seminary's *Narrative Lectionary*, http://www.workingpreacher.org/?lectionary=nl.

6. In the section that follows I survey a number of different types of sermon series that I have heard described by colleagues in ministry over the last ten years. I am especially indebted to Thomas Are Jr. at Village Presbyterian Church in Kansas City, Kansas; Otis Moss III at Trinity United Church of Christ in Chicago, Illinois; Agnes Norfleet at Bryn Mawr Presbyterian Church in Bryn Mawr, Pennsylvania; and Jon Walton at First Presbyterian Church in New York City for sharing their creative ideas.

7. Pew Research Center, "Public Sees Religion's Influence Waning: Growing Appetite for Religion in Politics," September 22, 2014, http://www.pewforum.org/files/2014/09/Religion-Politics-09-24-PDF-for-web.pdf. In this poll of over two thousand Americans, a majority indicated that they were interested in hearing their clergy speak out on controversial social issues while 63 percent stated that they did not want their clergy to endorse a particular candidate or party.

8. Thomas G. Long, *The Witness of Preaching*, 3rd ed. (Louisville, KY: Westminster John Knox Press, 2005), 4.

9. Ibid., 82.

CHAPTER 4. THE BLESSING OF MELCHIZEDEK

1. Robert Wuthnow, *America and the Challenges of Religious Diversity* (Princeton, NJ: Princeton University Press, 2005), 244.

2. Amy-Jill Levine, *Short Stories by Jesus: The Enigmatic Parables of a Controversial Rabbi* (San Francisco: HarperOne, 2014), 71–106.

3. Ibid., 94.

4. Jonathan Sacks, *The Dignity of Difference: How to Avoid the Clash of Civilizations* (New York: Continuum, 2002), 58.

5. Ibid., 21.

6. Ibid., 60.

CHAPTER 5. DISCERNING AUTHORITIES

1. Thomas G. Long, "Preaching Moment 139," Working Preacher, http://www.working preacher.org/craft.aspx?m=4377&post=2299.

2. Jean-François Lyotard, *The Postmodern Condition: A Report on Knowledge*, trans. Geoff Bennington and Brian Massumi (Minneapolis: University of Minnesota Press, 1984), xxiv–xxv.

3. Samuel D. Proctor, *The Certain Sound of the Trumpet: Crafting a Sermon of Authority* (Valley Forge, PA: Judson Press, 1994).

4. Olin P. Moyd, *The Sacred Art: Preaching and Theology in the African American Tradition* (Valley Forge, PA: Judson Press, 1995), 56

5. Cleophus J. LaRue, *I Believe I'll Testify: The Art of African American Preaching* (Louisville, KY: Westminster John Knox Press, 2011), 58, 64.

6. See Hannah Arendt, "What Is Authority?" in *Between Past and Future* (London: Penguin, 2006 (1954), 91–141.

7. Ibid., 105.

8. I offer a richer and more particular account of the transition from office to authenticity in Ted A. Smith, *The New Measures: A Theological History of Democratic Practice* (Cambridge: Cambridge University Press, 2007), chap. 5.

9. Gilbert Tennent, *The Danger of an Unconverted Ministry, Considered in a Sermon on Mark Vi. 34. Preached at Nottingham, in Pennsylvania, March 8. Anno 1739*, 40 (Philadelphia: Printed by Benjamin Franklin in Market-Street, 1740).

10. Fred B. Craddock, *As One without Authority*, 4th ed. (St. Louis: Chalice Press, 2001), 5.

11. Thomas G. Long, *The Witness of Preaching*, 3rd ed. (Louisville, KY: Westminster John Knox Press, 2016), 53.

12. Lori J. Carrell, *Preaching That Matters: Reflective Practices for Transforming Sermons* (Lanham, MD: Rowman & Littlefield, 2013), 131, emphasis original.

13. Anthony B. Robison, "How to Reach Young Adults," Faith and Leadership, https://www.faithandleadership.com/anthony-b-robinson-how-reach-young-adults.

14. Ed Stetzer and Jason Hayes, "Preaching to the Younger Unchurched," SermonCentral, http://www.sermoncentral.com/articleb.asp?article=Ed-Stezer-Jason-Hayes-Preaching-Younger-Unchurched.

15. Christine M. Smith, *Weaving the Sermon: Preaching in a Feminist Perspective* (Louisville, KY: Westminster John Knox Press, 1989), 46, 50, 51.

16. Anna Carter Florence, *Preaching as Testimony* (Louisville, KY: Westminster John Knox Press, 2007), xviii.

17. Ibid., 74.

18. See, for instance, Jodi Dean, "Donald Trump Is the Most Honest Candidate in American Politics Today," *In These Times*, http://inthesetimes.com/article/18309/donald-trump-republican-president; Doyle McManus, "Campaign 2016's Quixotic Quest for 'Authenticity,'" *Chicago Tribune*, http://www.chicagotribune.com/news/opinion/commentary/ct-bernie-sanders-donald-trump-authenticity-20151102-story.html; Rachel Stern, "Trump's Authenticity Is What's Making Him Popular, UB Political Scientist Says," University of Buffalo News Center, http://www.buffalo.edu/news/releases/2015/08/004.html.

19. When joined to a public role, what I have been calling "authenticity" becomes more like what I would call, following Lionel Trilling, "sincerity." Trilling's exploration of the two terms makes clear that each of them involves a kind of correspondence between the inner life of a person and some other point of reference. For sincerity, that point of reference is supplied by a public role or persona. For authenticity, however, that point of reference is supplied by a true or real self that is taken to be deep within a person. See Lionel Trilling, *Sincerity and Authenticity*, The Charles Eliot Norton Lectures (Cambridge, MA: Harvard University Press, 1972).

20. On the juxtaposition of private and public personae, see Michael Warner, "The Mass Public and the Mass Subject," in *Habermas and the Public Sphere*, ed. Craig Calhoun (Cambridge, MA: The MIT Press, 1992), 379–82.

21. See, for instance, Hendrik Hertzberg, "Spilled Oil," *The New Yorker*, June 28, 2010, http://www.newyorker.com/magazine/2010/06/28/spilled-oil.

22. Arlie Russell Hochschild, *The Managed Heart: Commercialization of Human Feeling*, 3rd ed. (Berkeley: University of California Press, 2012).

23. Michael Ignatieff, *Fire and Ashes: Success and Failure in Politics* (Cambridge, MA: Harvard University Press, 2013), 80–81.

24. For a helpful typology of contemporary forms of authority for preachers—and a concise statement of an important constructive proposal—see John S. McClure, *Preaching Words:*

144 Key Terms in Homiletics (Louisville, KY: Westminster John Knox Press, 2007), 7–10. I read McClure's *The Roundtable Pulpit: Where Leadership and Preaching Meet* (Nashville: Abingdon, 1995) and Lucy Atkinson Rose's *Sharing the Word: Preaching in the Roundtable Church* (Louisville, KY: Westminster John Knox Press, 1997) as two good proposals for generating the kind of authority that can come from democratic process.

CHAPTER 6. PREACHING IN MULTICULTURAL CONGREGATIONS

1. Evans E. Crawford, *The Hum: Call and Response in African American Preaching*, Abingdon Preacher's Library (Nashville: Abingdon Press, 1995).

2. L. Gregory Jones, "Traditioned Innovation" in *Faith & Leadership Journal*, January 20, 2009, https://www.faithandleadership.com/content/traditioned-innovation. Jones calls for a discernment process in leadership in order to decide what to hold on to and what to transform and what to affirm as people of God who have the "Reign of God" as their *telos*.

CHAPTER 8. PROPHESY TO THE BONES

1. Thomas G. Long and Thomas Lynch, *The Good Funeral: Death, Grief, and the Community of Care* (Louisville, KY: Westminster John Knox Press, 2013), 49.

2. Pew Research Center, "America's Changing Religious Landscape," May 12, 2015, http://www.pewforum.org/2015/05/12/new-pew-research-center-study-examines-americas-changing-religious-landscape/.

3. James F. Hopewell, *Congregation: Stories and Structures*, ed. Barbara Wheeler (Philadelphia: Fortress, 1987).

4. Hopewell, *Congregation*, 19–52; Long and Lynch, *The Good Funeral*, 49.

5. Hopewell, *Congregation*, 55–66.

6. Robert King, "Death and Resurrection of an Urban Church," *Faith and Leadership*, March 24, 2015, http://www.faithandleadership.com/death-and-resurrection-urban-church.

7. David Brooks, "Building Spiritual Capital," *New York Times*, May 22, 2015, http://www.nytimes.com/2015/05/22/opinion/david-brooks-building-spiritual-capital.html. Brooks is quoting psychologist Lisa Miller.

8. Ralph W. Klein, *Israel in Exile: A Theological Interpretation*, 2nd ed. (Philadelphia: Fortress, 1979), 108.

9. See Richard Lischer, *A Theology of Preaching: The Dynamics of the Gospel*, rev. ed. (Nashville: Abingdon, 2001), 10.

CHAPTER 9. LEARNING FROM AND TRANSFORMING THE COMMUNITY-BUILDING PROMISE OF SOCIAL NETWORKING SERVICES

1. Thomas G. Long, "Out of the Loop: The Changing Practice of Preaching," in *What's the Shape of Narrative Preaching? Essays in Honor of Eugene L. Lowry*, ed. Mike Graves and David Schlafer (St. Louis: Chalice Press, 2008), 115–30.

2. "Against Narrativity," in *Ratio* (new series) 27, no. 4 (Dec. 2004): 428–52.

3. Long, "Out of the Loop," 124.

4. Ibid., 126.

5. Ibid., 128.

6. John S. McClure, *Mashup Religion: Pop Music and Theological Invention* (Waco, TX: Baylor University Press, 2011).

7. Ibid., 127. I developed the idea of "nodes of complexity" in conversation with Vincent Miller's desire for more complex "building blocks" for those who are piecing their religious

ideas together in an online universe. Vincent J. Miller, *Consuming Religion: Christian Faith and Practice in a Consumer Culture* (London: A&C Black, 2005), 162, 176.

8. It was George Herbert Mead who first identified the significance of role-taking and role-playing for socialization into communities. For Mead, role-play is crucial for the construction of the social self. As the self takes roles for many others within a community, a "generalized other" emerges that defines the community's overall identity for the self. George Herbert Mead, *Mind, Self, and Society from the Perspective of the Social Behaviorist*, ed. Charles Morris (Chicago: University of Chicago Press, 1934). See also John H. Flavell, *The Development of Role-Taking and Communication Skills in Children* (Huntington, NY: Krieger Pub. Co., 1975).

9. See, for instance, Hubert Dreyfus, "Nihilism on the Information Highway: Anonymity versus Commitment in the Present Age," in *Community in the Digital Age: Philosophy and Practice*, ed. Andrew Feenberg and Darin Barney (Lanham, MD: Rowan and Littlefield, 2004), 69–81. See also Albert Borgmann, *Crossing the Postmodern Divide* (Chicago: University of Chicago Press, 1992).

10. M. Parsell, "Pernicious Virtual Communities: Identity, Polarisation and the Web 2.0," *Ethics and Information Technology* 10, no.1 (2008): 41.

11. Maria Bakardjieva and Georgia Gaden, "Web 2.0 Technologies of the Self," *Philosophy of Technology* 25, no. 3 (2011): 399–413.

12. Nelle Morton, *The Journey Is Home* (Boston: Beacon Press, 1985), 202–10.

13. Sherry Turkle, *Alone Together: Why We Expect More from Technology and Less from Each Other* (New York: Basic Books, 2011).

14. Andrew Keenan and Shiri Ali, "Sociability and Social Interaction on Social Networking Websites," *Library Review* 58, no. 6 (2009): 438–50.

15. Brian Carroll and Katie Landry, "Logging On and Letting Out: Using Online Social Networks to Grieve and to Mourn," *Bulletin of Science, Technology & Society* 30, no. 5 (October 1, 2010): 341–49.

16. For more on this idea of "divine empathy," see Edward Farley, *Divine Empathy: A Theology of God* (Minneapolis: Fortress Press, 1996).

17. Snapchat is currently the only form of social media that rebuffs archiving entirely, by allowing content to evaporate after it is shared. Because of this, it is, perhaps, the most truly "episodic" social media platform.

18. In Eliza Giaccardi, ed. *Heritage and Social Media: Understanding Heritage in a Participatory Culture* (New York: Routledge, 2012), xvi.

19. "Performance" refers to dramatic action or representation. "Performative" is a term taken from speech act theory that refers to words or ritual acts that are "self-referential" (about themselves) and "executive" (operate on themselves), creating in the moment that which is invoked. See J. L. Austin, "How to Do Things with Words, Lecture II" in *The Performance Studies Reader*, ed. Henry Bial (New York: Routledge, 2004), 147–54.

20. For more on kerygmatic and mimetic forms of memory, see John S. McClure, *Other-Wise Preaching: A Postmodern Ethic for Homiletics* (St. Louis: Chalice Press, 2001), 29–37.

21. See Gordon Lathrop, *Holy Things: A Liturgical Theology* (Minneapolis: Augsburg Fortress Press, 1998).

22. Thomas G. Long, *Preaching from Memory to Hope* (Louisville, KY: Westminster John Knox Press, 2009), 2009. See especially chap. 2, "No News Is Bad News: God in the Present Tense," 27–53.

23. Johann Baptist Metz, *Love's Strategy: The Political Theology of Johann Baptist Metz*, ed. John K. Downey (Harrisburg, PA: Trinity Press, 1999), 92.

24. See, for instance, Graham Murdoch, "Producing Consumerism: Commodities, Ideologies, Practices," in *Critique, Social Media and the Information Society*, ed. Christian Fuchs and Marisol Sandoval (New York: Routledge, 2013), 125–43.

25. Patrick Stokes, "Ghosts in the Machine: Do the Dead Live On in Facebook?" *Philosophy and Technology* 25, no. 3 (September 2012): 363–79.

26. Christopher Duraisingh, "From Church-Shaped Mission to Mission-Shaped Church," *Anglican Theological Review* 92, no. 1 (Winter 2010): 7–28.

27. Ibid., 7.

28. See, for instance, Antonio Marturano, "The Ethics of Online Social Networks—An Introduction," *International Review of Information Ethics* 16 (2011): 3–5.

29. Cass Sunstein, "Democracy and the Internet," in *Information Technology and Moral Philosophy*, eds. J. van den Hoven and J. Weckert (Cambridge: Cambridge University Press, 2008), 93–110.

30. Asaf Bar-Tura, *Facebook and Philosophy* (Chicago: Open Court, 2010), 239.

31. Nicholas Carr, *The Shallows: What the Internet Is Doing to Our Brains* (New York: Norton and Co., 2010).

32. For a good example of this rhythm, see Ruth A. Meyers, *Missional Worship, Worshipful Mission: Gathering as God's People, Going Out in God's Name* (Grand Rapids: Eerdmans, 2014).

33. The fundamental argument of my book *Mashup Religion* is that local worshipping congregations should avail themselves especially of the collaborative and inventive practices that are ubiquitous within popular culture today, much of which is fostered by social media.

CHAPTER 10. PROPHETIC TRUTH-TELLING IN A SEASON OF FATIGUE AND FRAGMENTATION

1. Thomas G. Long, *Witness of Preaching*, 3rd ed. (Louisville, KY: Westminster John Knox Press, 2016), 270.

2. Thomas G. Long, *The Senses of Preaching* (Atlanta: John Knox Press, 1988), 30–31.

3. "Justice fatigue" is a term I coined in 2012 to describe the urgency of addressing social ills even as we feel worn down due to constantly revisiting issues we thought were resolved, abject disappointment at the persistence of particular prejudices and oppressions, and frustration when one senses no one is listening.

4. Max Weber, *The Protestant Ethic and the Spirit of Capitalism,* trans. Talcott Parsons (New York: Charles Scribner's Sons, 1958), 254–55.

5. Steven Long, "Prophetic Preaching," in *Concise Encyclopedia of Preaching*, ed. William H. Willimon and Richard Lischer (Louisville, KY: Westminster John Knox Press, 1995), 388.

6. Thomas G. Long, "Preaching Moment 161," Working Preacher, https://www.workingpreacher.org/craft.aspx?m=4377&post=2300.

7. Long, *The Witness of Preaching*, 58.

8. Long, "Preaching Moment 161."

9. W. Paul Jones, *Worlds within a Congregation: Dealing with Theological Diversity* (Nashville: Abingdon Press, 2000), 36.

10. Charles Kelly, "Emphatic Listening," in *Small Group Communication*, ed. Robert S. Cathcart and Larry A. Samovar (Madison, WI: Brown and Benchmark Press, 1995), 296–97.

11. Samuel Dewitt Proctor and Gardner C. Taylor, *We Have This Ministry: The Heart of the Pastor's Vocation* (Valley Forge, PA: Judson Press, 1996), 118–26.

12. Molefi Kete Asante, "The Afrocentric Idea and the Cultural Turn in Intercultural Communication Studies" in *International Journal of Intercultural Relations* 36, no. 6 (November 2012): 760–69.

13. Teresa Fry Brown, "An African American Woman's Perspective" in *Preaching Justice: Ethnic and Cultural Perspectives*, ed. Christine M. Smith (Cleveland: United Church Press, 1998), 49.

14. Howard Thurman, *Luminous Darkness* (Richmond: Friends United Press, 1989), 100.

15. Teresa Fry Brown, "Hold onto Your Hope" (sermon, Samuel Dewitt Proctor Conference, Chicago, IL, February 2011); "Overcoming Justice Fatigue" (lecture, Princeton Seminary, Princeton, NJ, February 5, 2015).

16. Christine Smith, *Risking the Terror: Resurrection in This Life* (Cleveland: Pilgrim Press, 2001), 20–21.

17. Christine Smith, *Preaching as Weeping, Confession, and Resistance: Radical Responses to Radical Evil* (Louisville, KY: Westminster John Knox Press, 1992), 13.

18. Smith, *Risking the Terror*, 20–21.

19. Long, *The Senses of Preaching*, 28.

CHAPTER 11. TOMORROW'S BREAKING NEWS

1. In referring to "Pentecostal traditions," I have in mind not only churches that, in one way or another, trace their roots to American Pentecostalism as represented by the Azusa Street Revival led by William Seymour in Los Angeles in 1906 but a range of worshipping traditions that, historically, have emphasized embodied manifestations of the Holy Spirit's presence as the authenticating mark of Christian identity, worship, and preaching.

2. Eric Patterson and Edmund Rybarczyk, *The Future of Pentecostalism in the United States* (Lanham, MD: Rowan and Littlefield, 2007), 7–8.

3. Ibid., 202–6.

4. Ibid., 7–8.

5. Cheryl Bridges Johns, "What Makes a Good Sermon: A Pentecostal Perspective," *Journal for Preachers* 26, no. 4 (Pentecost, 2003): 51.

6. Cheryl Bridges Johns, "What Can the Mainline Learn from Pentecostals about Pentecost?" *Journal for Preachers* 21, no. 4 (Pentecost, 1998), 3–4, 5–6.

7. Scott Gibson, "Critique of the New Homiletic: Examining the Link between the New Hermeneutic and the New Homiletic," *Preaching Today* (August, 2005), http://www.preachingtoday.com/skills/2005/august/129--gibson.html.

8. United States Conference of Catholic Bishops, *Fulfilled in Your Hearing* (United States Conference of Catholic Bishops, 1982).

9. Karla J. Bellinger, *Connecting Pulpit and Pew: Breaking Open the Conversation about Catholic Preaching* (Collegeville, MN: Liturgical Press, 2014), 73–74. Bellinger's research revealed that some priests have an experience of being held at arm's length by their congregations and a sense they are living in a parallel culture.

10. Nancy Hilkert, *Naming Grace: Preaching and the Sacramental Imagination* (New York: Continuum, 1997).

11. United States Conference of Catholic Bishops, *Fulfilled in Your Hearing*, 20.

12. Guerric DeBona, *Fulfilled in Our Hearing: History and Method of Christian Preaching* (New York: Paulist Press, 2005), 28–77, 168–207.

13. O. Wesley Allen Jr., ed. *The Renewed Homiletic* (Minneapolis: Augsburg Fortress, 2010), 60.

14. Michel Foucault, *Power/Knowledge: Selected Interviews and Other Writings, 1972– 1977*, ed. Colin Gordon (New York: Pantheon, 1980), 133.

15. Some scholars in the field are cautious of the trust expressed here in the capacity of linguistic symbols to refer to the divine or divine action. For example, John McClure is cautious of the strong remnant of representational trust in the referentiality of symbols in an age in which reference has been deconstructed: "[T]he assumption that language serves an ontological function, that it discloses the being of things, can only be partly maintained, if at all." McClure, *Other-Wise Preaching: A Postmodern Ethic for Homiletics* (St. Louis: Chalice, 2001), 125. Postmodern-progressive preacher Phil Snider works along similar lines to McClure, stating, "God does not *exist*. God *insists*." Thus language is evocative but not referential and denotative. See Snider, *Preaching after God: Derrida, Caputo, and the Language of Postmodern Homiletics* (Eugene, OR: Cascade, 2012), 6, 46.

16. Penny Long Marler, et al., *So Much Better: How Thousands of Pastors Help Each Other Thrive* (St. Louis: Chalice, 2013), 3–4.

17. See Teresa Fry Brown, *Weary Throats and New Songs: Black Women Proclaiming God's Word* (Nashville: Abingdon, 2003); and Cleophus J. LaRue, *This Is My Story: Testimonies and Sermons of Black Women in Ministry* (Louisville, KY: Westminster John Knox Press, 2005).

18. For a brief introduction to the broad field of African American preaching, see Timothy Sensing, "African American Preaching," *Journal of the American Academy of Ministry* 7 (Winter/Spring 2001): 38–53.

19. Henry H. Mitchell, *Celebration and Experience in Preaching*, rev. ed. (Nashville: Abingdon, 2008); Gardner C. Taylor, *How Shall They Preach: The Lyman Beecher Lectures and Five Lenten Sermons* (Elgin, IL: Progressive Baptist Publishing, 1977); Samuel D. Proctor, *The Certain Sound of the Trumpet: Crafting a Sermon of Authority* (Valley Forge: Judson, 1994); James Earl Massey, *Stewards of the Story: The Task of Preaching* (Louisville, KY: Westminster John Knox Press, 2006); and James Henry Harris, *The Word Made Plain: The Power and Promise of Preaching* (Minneapolis: Augsburg Fortress, 2004).

20. Cleophus J. LaRue, *The Heart of Black Preaching*, 2nd ed. (Louisville, KY: Westminster John Knox Press, 2000); *I Believe I'll Testify: The Art of African American Preaching* (Louisville, KY: Westminster John Knox Press, 2011); Teresa Fry Brown, *Delivering the Sermon*, Elements of Preaching Series (Minneapolis: Fortress, 2008); Melva Wilson Costen, *African American Christian Worship*, 2nd ed. (Nashville: Abingdon, 2007); and Frank Thomas, *They Like to Never Quit Praisin' God: The Role of Celebration in Preaching*, rev. ed. (Cleveland: Pilgrim Press, 2013).

21. See Brian K. Blount, *Go Preach! God's Kingdom Message and the Black Church Today* (Maryknoll, NY: Orbis Books, 1998); *Can I Get a Witness: Reading Revelation through African American Culture* (Louisville, KY: Westminster John Knox Press, 2005); and *Invasion of the Dead: Preaching Resurrection* (Louisville, KY: Westminster John Knox Press, 2005).

22. Ralph Basui Watkins, *Hip-Hop Redemption: Finding God in the Rhythm and Rhyme* (Grand Rapids: Baker Academic, 2011).

23. Richard Lischer, *The Preacher King: Martin Luther King Jr. and the Word That Moved America* (New York: Oxford University Press, 1995) and Jared E. Alcantara, *Intercultural-Improvisational Homiletics in Conversation with Gardner C. Taylor* (Downers Grove, IL: IVP Academic, 2015).

24. One could argue that David Buttrick's preaching, unique among the New Homileticians, preserves the power of proposal-and-demonstration as the basic structure of its sequenced, episodic moves. See Allen, *Renewed Homiletic*, 15–16, 95.

25. See TED, "Our Organization," https://www.ted.com/about/our-organization.

26. Michael Toy, "Are TED Talks the New Sermon?" *Second Nature*, http://secondnaturejournal.com/are-ted-talks-the-new-sermon/.

27. Ibid.

28. Ibid.

29. Claudette Anderson Copeland, "Tamar's Torn Robe," in *This Is My Story: Testimonies and Sermons of Black Women in Ministry*, ed. Cleophus J. LaRue (Lousiville, KY: Westminster John Knox Press, 2005), 113–18. Copeland is cofounder of New Christian Fellowship and Destiny Ministries, San Antonio, Texas. The date and context of this sermon's presentation is not indicated by the editor.

30. "Soviet Jewelry," Vimeo video, 1:45, posted by Gal Beckerman, https://vimeo.com/9220868.

31. Michael Smith, "Ellen DeGeneres the Delicious Irony of Hosting Oscar Ceremony Again," *Liberty Voice*, August 3, 2013, http://guardianlv.com/2013/08/ellen-degeneres-the-delicious-irony-of-hosting-oscar-ceremony-again/.

32. Charles L. Campbell and Johann Cilliers, *Preaching Fools: The Gospel as a Rhetoric of Folly* (Waco, TX: Baylor University Press, 2012), 24–25.

33. Fred B. Craddock, "Enduring the Small Stuff," in *Ten Great Preachers: Message and Interviews*, ed. Bill Turpie (Grand Rapids: Baker, 2000), 49.

34. "FCCGE—'Home Economics'—Rev. Lillian Daniel," YouTube video, 30:30, from a sermon preached December 14, 2014, at First Congregational Church (UCC) of Glen Ellyn, Illinois, posted by 1stCongregationalGE, https://www.youtube.com/watch?v=xS9uQzJ7x7E&feature=youtu.be.

35. See, for example, archived chapel sermons by M. Craig Barnes, president of Princeton Theological Seminary, at https://www.ptsem.edu/index.aspx?id=25769807999&bnr=25769805108. Barnes regularly explores the ironies of the experience of Christian faith and Christian leadership, particularly our tendency to imagine that God is predictable or that Christian life and leadership is anything other than cruciform.

36. Toy, "Are TED Talks the New Sermon?"

CPSIA information can be obtained
at www.ICGtesting.com
Printed in the USA
LVHW080242280721
693900LV00023B/692